OF LEARNING
AND LIBRARIES:
THE SEMINARY LIBRARY
AT ONE HUNDRED

A CENTURY OF ACHIEVEMENT

1886–1986
תרמ"ו–תשמ"ו

OF LEARNING
AND LIBRARIES:
THE SEMINARY LIBRARY
AT ONE HUNDRED

by *Herman Dicker*

Foreword by
ISMAR SCHORSCH
Chancellor
Jewish Theological Seminary

A Centennial Publication of
The Jewish Theological Seminary of America
New York 1988

COPYRIGHT © 1988
THE JEWISH THEOLOGICAL SEMINARY OF AMERICA
Library of Congress Cataloging-in-Publication Data

Dicker, Herman, 1914–
    Of learning and libraries : the seminary library, at one hundred
by Herman Dicker ; foreword by Ismar Schorsch.
        p. cm.
    Bibliography: p.
    Includes index.
    ISBN 0-87334-045-0
    1. Jewish Theological Seminary of America. Library—History.
2. Rabbinical seminary libraries—New York (N.Y.)—History.
3. Jewish libraries—New York, (N.Y.)—History. 4. Jewish learning
and scholarship—New York (N.Y.)—History. I. Title.
Z733.J58D53   1987
027.6'3'08992409—dc 19   87-31944
                                                                        CIP

Contents

Illustrations

Foreword

Herman Dicker's charming history of the Seminary library is an exercise in metonymy. It must stand for a history of the entire institution. Unfortunately, the occasion of the Seminary's centennial failed to elicit or mobilize a thorough history of the institution within the context of American Judaism. We therefore doubly welcome the completion of this well-researched account of the library, which for the time being will have to serve as a partial view of a much larger vista.

To be sure, it is not a distorting angle of vision. A medieval monk once declared: "A monastery without a library is like a castle without an armory. Our library is our armory." From the very first, the library was at the core of the Seminary's self-image, its essential line of defense. The Seminary, especially as reorganized by Solomon Schechter, dared to expound an understanding of Judaism informed by the best of modern scholarship. Securing the future of Judaism in America meant recapturing the past—broadly, accurately, and empathetically. Toward the end, the assemblage of a great library housing the dazzling spectrum of Jewish literary creativity in the past and the ever widening circle of critical scholarship in the present was indispensable.

The goal loomed as a formidable challenge. Nineteenth-century Jewish philanthropy in Europe had been singularly unsuccessful in raising the funds necessary to transfer some of the great private Jewish collections into Jewish institutions. If *Wissenschaft des Judentum* (the scientific study of Judaism) was born on German soil, it is one of the ironies of its history that Jewish indifference in Germany permitted the three finest libraries of Jewish books and manuscripts in private hands in the country—those of David Oppenheimer, Heimann Joseph Michael, and Leeser Rosenthal—to be disposed of abroad. Leopold Zunz's sardonic quip about the Oppenheimer collection, which was purchased by the Bodleian Library of Oxford in 1829, applies aptly to the fate of all three: they "belong to the few memorials erected by Jews and preserved by Christians." By the late 1930's, the libraries of the three modern rabbinical schools in Germany had managed collectively to assemble barely 600 manuscripts, perhaps just as well.

That the library of the Seminary today comprises well over 11,000 manuscripts, always the most treasured part of any collection, is a glorious tribute to the original vision of its founders and the ongoing dedication of its donors. Decades before the specter of the Holocaust, they had combined to create a vast repository of the Jewish Experience in the new world. And at long last, their achievement is safely ensconced in a facility appropriate to its value and mission. An elegant blend of form and content, the Seminary library enters its second century as an urban oasis uniquely suited to sustain and refresh the Jewish religious and cultural imagination.

Introduction

by Menahem Schmelzer

During the Centennial Year of the Jewish Theological Seminary it is particularly fitting to publish an account of the Seminary library's birth, development, and growth. For this, gratitude is due Dr. Herman Dicker, former head of reader services at the library, who, since his retirement, has devoted much effort to the writing of such a chronicle, and which is a reflection of his careful research, dedication to Jewish cultural tradition, and great love for the Seminary library.

As the library enters its second century, it can look back with great pride upon its achievements which are so vividly portrayed by the author. Foremost among these is the fact that a collection of Judaica and Hebraica of such magnitude and diversity could be assembled at all; for the amassing of a collection that is internationally acknowledged as one of the most complete and valuable depositories of Jewish knowledge is in itself a major cause for rejoicing. Dr. Dicker reveals the motives and methods of the scholarly and lay leaders who labored so unselfishly in acquiring these treasurers, and these sections are the most exciting parts of his account. Equally important, though perhaps less dramatic, is the book's emphasis on the library's riches and its service to modern Jewish scholarship, a combination which has enabled twentieth-century Jewish scholars to produce seminal works. Moreover, the readiness of the library, during its century-long history, to open its gates to all who seek knowledge is generously acknowledged.

This extraordinary collection has lately been housed in a modern, attractive, convenient building which enhances the library's effectiveness in serving the public. The events leading to the construction of the new building are recorded in lively chapters, supplemented by "The Fire of '66," by Rabbi Barry D. Cytron, an eyewitness, and "The Prefab and the New Building," by Edith Degani, the diligent Assistant Librarian. A special vote of thanks is due to Dr. Michael Stanislawski of Columbia University, who has graciously permitted the reprinting of his scholarly essay on the Guenzburg library (see Appendix A). All these contributions illustrate most graphically the history of a remarkable institution, and make it possible for the public at large to capture the excitement which has accompanied the century of growth of the Seminary library.

As we look to the future, we hope that the library will enter a new stage in its development, for the immense variety of materials stored on its shelves will require a painstaking, scholarly, detailed catalog in order to do justice to the myriad pieces of information found in its treasures. Since the library's holdings cover a millennium, from the earliest medieval manuscript fragments until the most recent edition of a book on Yiddish poetry issued in South America, they represent, geographically and linguistically, the gamut of Jewish global experience. Thus, a catalog of all holdings would be most desirable. It would prove a great contribution to the understanding of Jewish life and events in Eastern and Western Europe, North Africa, the Near and Far East, and, of course, North and South America. Recording the riches contained in the library, however, requires time, the cooperation of many specialists, and the modern techniques of computerization. This, then, is the next great challenge facing the Seminary library, and we trust it will also be met, so that the second century of the library will be as glorious in achievements as the first.

Dr. Dicker's penetrating chronicle is tastefully illustrated by pictures of major personalities, events, and bookplates identifying the most important collections and their sponsors. To him, and his many contributors, whose assistance made this book possible, we express our heartfelt appreciation. This applies especially to Sharon Teitelbaum, whose sensitive editorial skill transformed a body of information into a lively story. May they all go from strength to strength.

Chapter One

The First Years: 1886–1902

A visitor to the busy campus of the Jewish Theological Seminary of America looks from its sturdy brick tower to its streamlined library and finds it difficult to imagine how matters stood at the Seminary's birth one hundred years ago.

A far different picture would have greeted a visitor on January 3, 1887, when the ten youngsters of the first preparatory class met in the vestry rooms of Congregation Shearith Israel at 5 West 19th Street. Little changed when, less than a year later, they moved to Cooper Union on Lafayette Street, where they remained until 1892. The fledgling school then made a move uptown, to a five-story brownstone purchased for it at 736 Lexington Avenue.

In 1902, fifteen years after its small beginnings in borrowed quarters, the Seminary first entered the Morningside Heights area, moving to 531 West 123rd Street. In 1929, the move to its present location at Broadway and 122nd Street took place.

The path marked by these changes shows more than an institution searching for better facilities. It shows, step by step, the process of building a center of Jewish learning in America.

FINDING A NEW WAY

Without a library, indeed a great library, this goal could not have been achieved. The story of how this library came to be is part of the communal drama leading to the incorporation of the Jewish Theological Seminary Association in 1886 and its reorganization as the Jewish Theological Seminary of America in 1902.

The circumstances that led to the founding of the Seminary have been treated in depth elsewhere[1] and need only a short recapitulation here. In brief, the Seminary was the most serious response of traditional Jews to the organizational and polemical successes of the American Reform movement.

Reform came to America in the middle of the nineteenth century, brought from Europe by rabbis coming to serve American congregations. By attending universities as well as rabbinical seminaries, these rabbis had been influenced by the Enlightenment, the liberal ideology that had triumphed in the French Revolution and then swept through Central Europe.

Eager to break out of the ghetto and speed Jewish integration into general society, some rabbis began to reinterpret the traditional teachings of Judaism. These new interpretations led to reforms in the synagogue service, such as the inclusion of prayers in the German language and the use of organ music. Reform also transformed the role of the rabbi from that of the authority on Jewish law to preacher and educator of youth. Moreover, it encouraged the rabbi to become active in communal and even political affairs.

The individual most closely associated with the new movement was Isaac Mayer Wise (1819–1900). Born in Bohemia, he came to America in 1846, serving briefly as a rabbi in Albany, New York, and then moving to Cincinnati's Congregation Bene Yeshurun, to which he devoted the remaining forty-six years of his busy life. Thanks to him, Cincinnati became the main address of American Reform. To him as well is owed the existence of the pillars of American Reform: the Union of American Hebrew Congregations, founded in 1873, and Hebrew Union College, established two years later.

Interestingly, in view of subsequent tensions, Rabbi Wise's more traditional colleagues supported his efforts to organize the scattered congregations and provide them with rabbis. Sabato Morais, soon to become the rallying point for opponents of

Reform, even served as head of the college's board of examiners.[2] Privately, he may have hoped that his support would induce Wise to stay on a course acceptable to the traditionalists. However, the rabbinic conference held at Pittsburgh in 1885 effectively dashed such hopes. That conference, with its radically Reform platform, was a turning point in American Jewish history.

The tenets of the Pittsburgh Platform came to be known as classical American Reform. In essence, the platform echoed the Reform rabbis in Germany, who stressed the primacy of ethics and morality over the requirements of laws and rituals. It rejected all religious ceremonies which were not adaptable to modern mores. The fourth of the platform's eight terse paragraphs was especially provocative. It read:

> We hold that all Mosaic and Rabbinical laws as regulate diet, priestly purity, and dress, originated in ages and under the influence of ideas altogether foreign to our present mental and spiritual state. They fail to impress the modern Jew with a spirit of priestly holiness; their observance in our days is apt rather to obstruct than to further modern spiritual elevation.[3]

The principal author of the document was Kaufmann Kohler (1843–1926). Kohler hailed from Fuerth, a stronghold of traditionalism in southern Germany, and received his rabbinic training from the most orthodox rabbis, including Samson Raphael Hirsch (1808–1888) of Frankfurt-Main. But, like many of his generation, he veered from the traditional path after being exposed to a university education. His critical approach to Bible and Talmud made it impossible for him to obtain a rabbinic position at home, forcing him to emigrate to America. There he made his mark as one of the most important Reform leaders of his time.

He was soon to meet his match. The sharp position of the Pittsburgh Platform propelled the traditional forces into concerted action. Their champion was Sabato Morais (1823–1897), rabbi of a prestigious Sephardic congregation, Mikveh Israel of

Philadelphia. After a period of intense debate, the traditionalists agreed to the establishment, in 1886, of the Jewish Theological Seminary Association.

Like the delegates at Pittsburgh, the writers of the Seminary's constitution did not mince words. The goals of the new Seminary were stated as follows:

> The necessity has been made manifest for associated and organized effort on the part of the Jews of America faithful to Mosaic law and ancestral traditions, for the purpose of keeping alive the true Judaic spirit; in particular by the establishment of a seminary where the Bible shall be impartially taught and rabbinical literature faithfully expounded, and more especially where youths, desiring of entering the ministry, may be thoroughly grounded in Jewish knowledge and inspired by love of the Hebrew language, and a spirit of fidelity and devotion to the Jewish law.[4]

Defining further the objectives of the Seminary, Rabbi Morais, then president of the faculty, said:

> At the basis of our Seminary, lies the belief that Moses was in all truth inspired by the living God to promulgate laws for the government of a people sanctified to an imprescriptible mission; that the laws, embodied in the Pentateuch, have unavoidably a local and general application. Those comprised in the first category lose their force outside of Palestine, the other are obligatory elsewhere; but both the former and the latter, being of necessity broadly formulated, needed in all ages an oral interpretation. The traditions of the fathers are therefore coequal with the written statutes of the five holy books.[5]

In the early years, support for the Seminary's position came from several able spokesmen. Foremost among them was Alexander Kohut (1842–1894), a Hungarian rabbi who had arrived in New York in 1884 to serve as spiritual leader of Congregation Ahawath Chesed.[6] The descendant of a rabbinical family, Kohut had obtained his training in Budapest and at the Rabbinical Seminary of Breslau, Germany, under Zacharias Frankel (1801–1875). A great scholar—he completed his multivolume dictionary of Talmudic terms, *Aruch Hashalem*, in New York—he was also an eloquent speaker who challenged in speech and print the views of Reform's principal spokesman, Kaufmann Kohler.

As a follower of the historical approach to Judaism taught by Frankel, Kohut believed in making changes in "non-essential" religious practices to enhance the piety of the congregation. But these changes had to be based upon the Torah as interpreted by rabbinical law, and introduced by learned men. Kohut argued: "A Reform which seeks to progress without the Mosaic-rabbinical tradition is a deformity—a skeleton without flesh and sinew, without spirit and heart. It is suicide."[7] And further: "If we would burn the bridges behind us which unite the present with the past and yield to every whim for change propagandized by irresponsible religious leaders, our end would be chaos and death."[8] Kohut served as professor of Talmud at the Seminary, but his work as a teacher and spokesman for traditional Judaism was cut short by his early death.

LAYING THE FOUNDATIONS

With the Seminary's intellectual ground staked out, other critical institutional decisions—about location, faculty, and resources—could fall into place.

Recognizing early the importance of starting a comprehensive library collection, the Seminary leadership appointed a special committee to begin this work at once. Despite adequate resources and a clear mandate, the committee was stopped short by the scarcity of books for advanced Jewish studies. Most of the Hebrew publications to date were congregational prayerbooks and elementary-school texts, hardly the resource material required by advanced seminarians. In a promising development, the Jewish Publication Society of America began functioning again in 1888, despite two previous unsuccessful starts, but it would take some years for this Philadelphia society to produce material useful to students preparing for the rabbinate.[9]

At first, the library depended on donations from knowledgeable individuals. One of the earliest donors was Cyrus Adler (1863–1940), whose understanding of books helped guide the library from his first involvement as a young scholar until his death while the Seminary's third president.[10] Adler's ties to the Seminary were cemented by his lifelong admiration for Rabbi Morais and his connection to staunch Seminary supporters, the Sulzbergers of Philadelphia.

From his birthplace of Van Buren, Arkansas, Adler had been brought to Philadelphia as a young child by his mother, a member of the Sulzberger family, when she was widowed at the age of twenty-eight. The Sulzbergers had arrived from southern Germany during the middle of the nineteenth century and, being traditionally oriented, had become members of Rabbi Morais's synagogue, Mikveh Israel.

After graduating from the University of Pennsylvania in 1883, Adler first thought of becoming a lawyer. He started in that profession with his cousin Mayer Sulzberger (1843–1923), a distinguished jurist who was to play a leading role in the development of the Seminary and its library. But Adler soon turned instead to the field of Oriental studies, enrolling in Johns Hopkins University in Baltimore, which awarded him a doctorate in 1887. He then accepted a position as instructor in Semitics at the university, and also served as a director of the Ancient Near East Department of the Washington National Museum. In 1893, he was made a librarian at the Smithsonian Institution, and became its assistant secretary in 1905.

His background in Oriental studies and his sense of obligation to the Jewish community drew him to the institution headed by his teacher, Morais. And, indeed, in the very first *Proceedings* of the Seminary (1888), Adler's name appears as the donor of books to the young library.

Still, the task at hand overwhelmed the meager resources available in America. Of necessity, the library committee made overtures to private collectors in Europe, in the hope that personal libraries might become available for purchase. The strategy paid off in 1893, in the library's first major acquisition— 3,000 volumes from the holdings of Dr. David Cassel, a German scholar.

Also in 1893 Sabato Morais celebrated his seventieth birthday.

In his honor, the library was named the Sabato Morais Library. A few years later, in 1897, Morais willed his personal collection of 700 volumes for the use of faculty and students.

But the most significant early contribution to the young library was made by Adler's cousin, Mayer Sulzberger. His private collection, acquired over the years, would propel the Seminary library to national and international prominence. Perhaps more importantly, Sulzberger played a singular role in persuading Solomon Schechter to lead the institution of which the library was such an important part.

Prominent as a lawyer and judge, outstanding as a leader in Jewish communal affairs, bachelor Sulzberger seems to have devoted all his considerable energies to his profession and his community.[11] His commitment to Judaism was inspired first by his father, a teacher and a cantor, and reinforced by Isaac Leeser and Sabato Morais, rabbis of his synagogue, Mikveh Israel. When they organized the first rabbinical college, the short-lived Maimonides College, Sulzberger served as its secretary.

Concerned with raising the level of Jewish education within the community, the young lawyer founded Philadelphia's Young Men's Hebrew Association (YMHA), which provided a general meeting ground for educational and social programs, and became its first president. In 1888, when the Jewish Publication Society of America commenced operations for the third time, Sulzberger chaired its publication committee, lending it scope and stability.

In the course of his travels, Sulzberger met Solomon Schechter (1850–1915), reader in Rabbinics at Cambridge University and future head of the Seminary. Arriving in London in 1882 from his native Rumania, Schechter soon made his reputation with his scholarly teaching and writing. His charm and hospitality attracted many important visitors from America.[12]

Eager to introduce Schechter to America, Sulzberger, together with Dr. Solomon Solis-Cohen (1857–1948), a physician and fellow member of Philadelphia's traditional elite, invited the scholar to give a series of lectures in Philadelphia. The occasion was the establishment of Gratz College (1895), founded to train

Jewish teachers. While in the United States, Schechter stayed in Sulzberger's home, which he described, humorously, as "a little paradise on earth. I wonder whether they have such a nice library in the Garden of Eden, so many novels and so little theology."[13] On this visit, Schechter became acquainted with the aging Morais, who hoped, as did others, that Schechter could be persuaded to come to New York permanently.

This prospect required seven years of negotiations to materialize,[14] and Sulzberger was indispensable in achieving the happy result. During the protracted negotiations, Schechter came to rely upon him almost exclusively. This is evident from his letters to the judge, which reveal the extent of their shared interests and close friendship.[15]

Through these letters, the two men exchanged views and friendly services. As chairman of the Publication Society's publication committee, Sulzberger was very helpful in getting Schechter's *Studies in Judaism* published in the United States. Schechter, knowing that Sulzberger was a great collector of books, advised his friend on what to buy; in turn, Schechter received hard-to-get American novels from his Philadelphia connection.[16]

The letters also introduce Schechter's views on Judaism. He entered the heated debate on modern Judaism as an independent thinker, refusing to frame his views in a partisan manner. Commenting on his *Studies*, he writes: "There are indeed passages in the Book which neither the orthodox nor the reformers will find to their liking, as I belong to neither set."[17] In considering a permanent move to America he emphatically made it clear that his goal was "not to save orthodoxy, but Judaism."[18]

The correspondence contains Schechter's surprising initial assessment of his major scholarly find. Early in 1897, Schechter spent several weeks in Cairo, Egypt, collecting thousands of fragments from the synagogue's century-old storage attic, or *Genizah*. This expedition would assure his place in the annals of historical discoveries, but at the time he did not seem to realize the significance of the treasures he had found. He wrote to Sulzberger:

It was a hard piece of work; for weeks and weeks I had to swallow the dust of the centuries which nearly suffocated and blinded me (I am now undergoing medical treatment) and the annoyance with those scoundrels of whom I had to bakshish constantly. The manuscripts—all consisting of fragments—are now on their way to England. They number by thousands and there is a good deal of useless matter among them, but also some good things. It was impossible to examine them here (the Genizah being rather dark and dusty) and thus my policy was to take everything I could.[19]

WOOING SCHECHTER

With Sabato Morais ailing, Schechter had been approached confidentially by an unidentified correspondent to come to New York and assume the chancellorship of the Seminary. About this overture, he wrote his confidant, Sulzberger:

I have not answered him yet; but I am going to refer him to you. I hardly need tell you that America has certain attractions for me. But I am, of course, anxious to be there quite independent as well as sure of doing there something good by founding there a school on a scientific basis. You probably know what I want or rather what I ought to want better than I myself. Hence, the best thing that you decide for me in this respect.[20]

The warmth between the two friends is revealed again in a subsequent letter, dated August 5, 1887: "When you will tell me that the matter is worth considering, then we (you first) will consider it. Why do they [not] put the College in Philadelphia. This would be 'himmlisch' [celestial]."[21]

Schechter's hesitation was due to a variety of factors. On the one hand, his situation in Cambridge was not entirely satisfactory; on the other hand, the situation in New York was full of uncertainty. Coming from a Chassidic family in a small community in Rumania, he felt uncomfortable in the Christian environment of academic Cambridge. Thus he mused to Sulzberger: "You see I become mystical; a feeling which always overcomes me on the eve of our festivals which I must spend here among non-Jews, without synagogue and without Jewish friends. And what shall become of my children in this wilderness."[22]

When he wrote about wanting to be independent, he added parenthetically the words "Parnassa bekavod," Hebrew for "Income with Honor." His lecturer's salary at Cambridge could not have been adequate for a growing family with three children. On one occasion, Schechter apologizes for neglecting to mail a letter to America in order to save postage, "which become sometimes a heavy tax on me."[23] But he did not expect any increase in salary, despite his years of "killing work" and his great reputation. When word of his interest in an American position circulated, talk of trying to keep Schechter by offering him a professorship at the University of London immediately followed.[24]

The independence Schechter desired involved not only an adequate salary but also authority in the selection of teachers, the supervision of their work, and the granting of degrees. In these matters he was apprehensive about a move to New York. At the Seminary, some of these functions had been discharged by an advisory board of rabbis, and Schechter's past experience led him to question the practice of granting congregational leaders academic authority at a school dedicated to the Science of Judaism. He wrote bluntly:

> Our platform Rabbis are the destruction of Jewish learning, and their parish work leaves them no time for study. It is not much better in England. We have not a single minister who does or even cares for scholarly work. My hope for the future of Judaism and its literature is in America.[25]

He also was concerned about the Seminary's finances. Up until 1902, the Seminary's funds were donated by individuals and by the Seminary Associations of Philadelphia, Baltimore, and Syracuse. According to the report of the Biennial Convention of 1902, the total income for the two-year period amounted to a little more than $10,000, of which fully one-tenth came from Kuhn, Loeb and Company, the investment firm headed by Jacob H. Schiff.

Schechter may have been wary that Schiff, a member of the Reform congregation of Temple Emanu-El, would interfere with his traditionalist position. This apprehension may have been fanned by his negative experiences with wealthy circles in England. He writes about his war with "our Anglo-Saxons of Mosaic persuasion" on the issues of Zionism and Russian Jewry:

> I do not preach Zionism; but it is high time to strengthen the Jewish consciousness of which our stock-exchange chaplains were steadily working away. It was also high time to tell them that millions do not compensate us for their ignorance and that they have no right to any claim of intellectual and spiritual superiority over their brethren abroad, particularly the Russian Jews whom they are always bullying.[26]

Schechter was pleased and reassured when Sulzberger characterized Schiff as a "conservative reformer."[27] Indeed, it was Schiff who, together with his friends Leonard Lewisohn (1847-1902) and Daniel Guggenheim (1856-1930), donated $200,000 towards the $1 million endowment considered necessary to keep the Seminary solvent.[28]

Not only Schechter's misgivings needed to be stilled. Schiff and other patrons of the Seminary also needed assurances. It was Cyrus Adler, enjoying the confidence of all parties, who was the key to making the deal.[29] For Schechter, Adler was able to guarantee that Schechter's position as president of the faculty included the necessary academic authority. For Schiff, Adler agreed reluctantly, to oversee the new Seminary administration as president of the board of trustees. This was a pivotal role: Adler could use his contacts with influential members of the Jewish community to garner the financial resources and popular support needed to carry out Schechter's program; his assumption of the manifold details of management would leave Schechter free to teach and study; as a scholar, he could be counted on to stand up, if necessary, against outside meddling in the academic affairs of the Seminary.

All the arrangements, particularly those of a financial nature, were duly recorded on October 28, 1901, paving the way for Schechter's formal election as president of the faculty. Adler was appointed president of the board of trustees, and Louis Marshall (1856-1929), chairman of the executive committee.[30] Henceforth the Seminary was to be known as the Jewish Theological Seminary of America. And the stage was set for the principal character to appear on the scene in the person of Solomon Schechter, who arrived in New York on April 17, 1902.

SCHECHTER TAKES CHARGE

Dr. Louis Finkelstein, the fourth president of the Seminary (now retired), has called Solomon Schechter one of the foremost personalities of post-Talmudic times.[31] Coming from such an eminent source, this evaluation is so encompassing that if we were to add to it, to paraphrase a Talmudic saying, we would only diminish its value. Still, in seeking to understand Schechter's enormous impact, it would be helpful to focus on the convictions that characterized his leadership.

In the preface to his *Seminary Addresses*, Schechter describes the essays as a plea for traditional Judaism. He advocated a stricter observance of the precepts of the Torah, alerting all to the dangers of "incessant innovations which must in the end touch the very vital organism of Judaism." In all this, he saw the Seminary's role as one of teaching and preaching. Deploring the "shock-tactics" of Biblical Criticism, then an academic vogue, he demanded a rigorous academic method for studying Jewish thought, rooted in the analysis of Jewish texts.

The impact of these views on Seminary policy was evident in Schechter's handling of his first task—finding a faculty. In the past, the teaching program at the Seminary had been a limited one, with instruction carried out mainly by congregational rabbis with a scholarly background. But Schechter was more demanding: he wanted to hire recognized scholars who were traditional Jews and willing to be full-time instructors. He successfully recruited several such outstanding individuals early in their careers who later were to become celebrated as scholars.

One example was Louis Ginzberg (1873-1953), a master of both Talmudic knowledge, acquired in Lithuanian yeshivot, and scientific training, received in German universities. Before coming to America in 1899, he had been promised a position at the Hebrew Union College in Cincinnati which, for personal rea-

sons, he did not assume.[32] Schechter appointed Ginzberg professor of Talmud—but kept one course, "Introduction into the Old
Testament," for himself because "he could not trust anyone with
it."[33]

For professor of Biblical literature, Schechter hired Israel
Friedlaender (1876-1920), then a well-known instructor at the
University of Strassburg but formerly a student at the traditional Hildesheimer Rabbinical Seminary in Berlin. Signifi-
cantly, after enumerating his scholarly achievements in great
detail, Schechter said: "I may add that Israel Friedlaender is
strictly conservative in his life."[34]

Equally suitable on all fronts was Alexander Marx (1878-
1954). He too had turned away from a rabbinical career to study
history and bibliography. Marx became professor of history,
with the proviso that he would work five hours daily in the
library as acting chief librarian. In his eulogy of Mathilde
Schechter, Marx gives credit to her for having directed her
husband's attention to him for the postion in New York,[35] but
certainly it was Schechter alone who persuaded Marx's father,
an affluent banker from Koenigsberg, to allow the young man to
come to New York. The elder Marx dispatched a telegram to
Schechter, which read: "In the event that your Seminary is
firmly based on tradition and only teaches according to your
concept, I have no objections to Alexander's entry."[36]

Another example of Schechter's desire to obtain full-time
instructors was the appointment of Israel Davidson (1870-1939),
destined to become famous as the author of the four-volume
Thesaurus of Medieval Hebrew Literature. Davidson had to agree to
give up his position as chaplain of Sing Sing, a penal institution,
so that he could devote ten to twelve hours a week to teaching,
which "might not collide with his literary work."[37]

In some cases, Schechter loosened his strict requirements to
keep on the faculty individuals with other assets. Rabbi Bernard
Drachman (1861-1945), one of the original founders of the
Seminary and a member of its faculty since its inception, had
expected to be offered a professorship, but since Drachman, a
busy congregational rabbi, was available for a limited number of

hours, he was offered only a lectureship.[38] Schechter had been under pressure to dismiss him altogether but had resisted. First, he did not consider it fair to summarily dismiss a man who had been at a post for fifteen years. Secondly, Drachman was the only American graduate on the faculty and could help the Seminary with his "kosher" English. Thirdly, Drachman could bring the Seminary closer to Schechter's ideal as a learning center for all segments of Jewish society. Schechter particularly wanted to meet the religious needs of the "downtown" Jews, that is, the masses of Russian immigrants who lived on the East Side of Manhattan. The Seminary, with its supporters mainly re-cruited from the German-Jewish circles, was considered "up-town," but Drachman had a large following "downtown" and was an important link to the people Schechter desired to reach. Still, in 1909, Drachman left the Seminary altogether, claiming that "it had departed from the views of Sabato Morais."

While Schechter was carefully building his faculty, Jacob Schiff was preparing a new home for the Seminary. In a gesture whose timing underlined the new beginnings underway, Schiff and his wife, Therese, donated the new building on November 20, 1902, the day of Schechter's inauguration as president of the faculty. This meant transferring the institution from its mid-town location to Morningside Heights, an area where other academic establishments were already located. The Seminary's association with these other institutions, including Columbia University, Teachers College, Barnard College, and the Union Theological Seminary, would prove mutually beneficial.

At the dedication of the new building on April 26, 1903, Schiff stated that the Seminary had but one single purpose: to be an institution for all desiring to prepare for the Jewish ministry. He added, pointedly:

> While Judaism in America, not as it is so frequently misnamed, American Judaism, is particularly destined to continue the evolution which forever has been going forward in our religion, this cannot be accomplished by the radical tearing down process which during recent decades has made such unchecked headway.[39]

These observations indicated Schiff's opposition to the excesses of Reform, and explain his lifelong support of the Seminary.

In Schechter's own remarks on this occasion, which he considered important enough to include in his *Seminary Addresses*, the new president of the faculty enlarged upon Schiff's ideas.

> The Directors of this institution, by terming it the Jewish Theological Seminary of America have distinctly shown their intention of avoiding sectarianism. . . . The large bulk of the real American people have, in matters of religion, retained their sobriety and loyal adherence to the Scriptures, as their Puritan forefathers did. America stands both for wideness of scope and for conservatism. But be this as it may, forget not that this is a *Jewish* Theological Seminary, having the mission to teach the doctrines and the literature of the religion which is as old as history itself and as wide as the world. Any attempt to confine its activity to the borders of a single country, even be it as large as America will only make its teachings provincial, narrow and unprofitable. Israel, and Israel alone, must be the end for which synagogues and seminaries are erected, even in this country.[40]

On that day, Mayer Sulzberger's words spoke most directly to the dream of establishing a major Jewish library under Seminary auspices. What the judge said was, in essence, an amplification of the Seminary's charter, which included the establishment of a library as one of its goals. Following are some of his remarks:

> So far as we know, there were about one hundred Hebrew books printed during the first twenty-five years after the Hebrew press was started, that is, from the year 1475 to the year 1500, and these were produced mainly in Italy, the smaller number in Spain and Portugal. After its expulsion from Spain and Portugal, the Hebrew press sought refuge in Turkey, a few years later in Bohemia, and later still in Germany, Poland, Holland and other countries, until in modern times it has been established in nearly every land.
>
> That a complete collection of these books will ever be made in any library of the world is too much to hope. The books, like their owners, underwent so many persecutions, expulsions and burnings that the relatively small editions of early times were exhausted by drastic means. Moreover, in comparing the early books of general literature with the early Hebrew books, the fact will be noted that

while general works of the early age can be found in perfect
condition, the same is not often true of Hebrew books. The former
give evidence that many of them were placed in stately libraries and
daintily cared for, while the latter show hard and incessant usage.
The Gentiles read their books, the Jews devoured theirs.

The Bodleian Library at Oxford and the British Museum at
London are, and perhaps will always remain, the most magnificent
and complete Hebrew book museums in the world. But it is our
business on this side of the Atlantic to hope and work, undaunted by
the magnitude of others' achievements; we should hold in view the
purpose to make our collection as nearly complete as the resources of
the world may render possible, and in so doing we should spare
neither thought nor labor nor money. Closely related to the acquisition of printed books is the acquisition of manuscripts of works,
printed or unprinted. All that may be said in favor of the early
printed books applies to manuscripts, and the latter have this
additional qualification, that they sometimes serve to correct important errors in the printed books, just as the first editions of the
printed books serve to correct important errors introduced purposely
or inadvertently into later editions.[41]

Chapter Two

The Schechter Era: 1902–1915

The library began to take shape as the new Seminary administration settled in. With its objectives spelled out and its staff of
one, Alexander Marx, in place, the library entered a period of
growth which would bring it renown within ten years.

THE SULZBERGER COLLECTION

Seminary patron Mayer Sulzberger launched this period with a
major donation to the library. As his remarks at the dedication
ceremony show, he had spent many years considering and
collecting precious books and manuscripts from all over the
world. When he spoke on that occasion, his personal library
numbered about 2,400 rare books and 500 manuscripts, but he
must have then been in the process of acquiring 5,500 books and
200 manuscripts from the library of S. Halberstamm (1832–
1900) of Bielitz, Austria.

While Schechter was still in Cambridge, Sulzberger wrote
him of his intention to donate this valuable collection to the
library—news which Schechter welcomed warmly, expressing
the hope that the Seminary would prove itself worthy of such a
gift.[1]

Between Sulzberger's letter to England and his letter of January 20, 1904, to the Seminary board announcing his gift of 7,500
printed books and about 750 manuscripts, final details of the
Halberstamm acquisition were ironed out. The consummation
of the deal depended, in the end, on the judgment of Alexander

Marx, who fortunately was still in Germany. In a letter dated
August 10, 1903, Sulzberger asked Marx to proceed to Bielitz
and examine the library of Halberstamm, for which a price of
10,000 marks had been agreed on. If Marx's appraisal was
positive, the sum would be paid by Judge Sulzberger to a Dr.
Leo Halberstamm (presumably the son of the collector).[2]

The Sulzberger collection became a cornerstone of the Seminary library. All that Sulzberger asked was that each volume
contain his bookplate and, at a later date, he or his legal
representative be allowed to place the Hebrew books of his
father and grandfather in a separate case in the library.[3]

In building his collection, Sulzberger relied on the assistance
of Ephraim Deinard, businessman, scholar, traveler, author, and
publisher.[4] A Russian, Deinard enjoyed a solid reputation as one
who traveled far and wide in search of material. He then sold his
finds to the leading libraries and private collectors of Europe. He
also published, in Hebrew, many books about his travels and
discoveries.

After his arrival in America in 1888, Deinard continued in his
role as middleman between rare books and connoisseurs. One of
his major clients was Judge Sulzberger, about whose library he
published, in Hebrew, an annotated catalog in 1896.[5] The
catalog also documents Sulzberger's collection of religious objects, which he gave to the Seminary's museum. Of special
interest is a Torah scroll from the ancient community of Kai-
Feng-Fu in China.[6] Of course, the Deinard catalog enumerates
only those items in the collection at the time of its publication.
With the help of Deinard, Sulzberger continued to stock the
Seminary library until his death in 1923.

THE ROLE OF ALEXANDER MARX

Schechter's invitation to Alexander Marx to come to New York
and become professor of history and librarian must have struck
the young man as a great honor, but ultimately the honor
redounded to the Seminary. For Marx was a brilliant choice, and
he more than lived up to the promise Schechter had recognized
so early.

Schechter had been following Marx's progress since their meeting in Cambridge in 1898, when Marx consulted him in his search for manuscripts of the Hebrew historical chronicle, *Seder Olam*. Like others seriously seeking Hebrew manuscripts or early prints, sooner or later Marx had to come to the great English libraries: the British Museum of London and the Bodleian of Oxford. Marx surely knew that Schechter, then at the height of his Genizah fame, had copied some important manuscripts on *Seder Olam*, with the thought of editing a critical edition. About his visit to Schechter, Marx wrote, "Without hesitation he presented all his material, the result of considerable work, to the young stranger, of whom he knew nothing."[7]

Another bond between the mature scholar and his young colleague was their mutual acquaintance with and respect for Moritz Steinschneider (1816–1907) of Berlin. Schechter knew him from his own studies in that city, and Marx called him his "revered master." Steinschneider, who is generally considered the father of modern Jewish bibliography, had been writing and teaching in Berlin for more than two generations, and many of his students became prominent scholars. Both Schechter and Marx had written glowing tributes to him.[8]

Steinschneider was familiar with the holdings of all the major European libraries. His greatest bibliographic work, *Catalog of Hebrew Books in the Bodleian Library*, documented that library's collection up to 1732.[9] We find the Steinschneider preoccupation with manuscripts and research in all scholars guided by the principles of *Wissenschaft*, the "science of Judaism," that is, the study of Judaism according to documentary evidence. We see it in Schechter, whose aim was to establish a center of *scientific* learning in America. His commitment to this concept was clearly stated in his inaugural address of November 2, 1902.

Every discovery of an ancient document giving evidence of a bygone world is, if undertaken in the right spirit—that is for the honor of God and the truth and not for the glory of self—an act of resurrection in miniature. But it is with truth as it is with other ideals and sacred possessions of man. Every generation, [Schechter gives a Rabbinic quotation], which did not live to see the rebuilding of the

Holy Temple must consider itself as if it had witnessed its destruction. Similarly, we may say that every age which has not made some essential contribution to the erection of the Temple of Truth and real *Wissenschaft* is bound to look upon itself as if it had been instrumental in its destruction.[10]

A few years later, Schechter again took up the subject of "Jewish *Wissenschaft*," demonstrating that many of our luminaries could have made an even greater contribution had they more manuscripts at their disposal.[11] With deep respect, he points to Rabbi Elijah, the "Gaon" of Vilna (1720–1797), who, working with very few manuscripts, was able to interpret texts so profoundly only because of his unparalleled mastery of the printed material that was available. Likewise, historians Leopold Zunz (1794–1886) and Heinrich Graetz (1817–1891) could have accomplished more with access to libraries with more manuscripts and documents.

Marx, Steinschneider's outstanding student, shared with Schechter this particular approach to scholarship. In addition, Marx came from an observant home and had studied at the traditional Hildesheimer Rabbinical Seminary. (Indeed, its rector, Dr. David Hoffmann (1843–1921), would become his father-in-law.) Schechter believed that Marx, like Hoffmann, would be able to combine scientific methods of scholarship with pious dedication to tradition.[12]

Before officially assuming his Seminary duties in the fall of 1903, Marx was given a special assignment: Schechter, writing to Marx from New York of how anxiously he and his wife were looking forward to his arrival, added, "If it would not prove too much trouble to you, I should like to ask you to bring us four more of the teaspoons you helped me buying *(sic)* in Berlin. If you find something of a more practical sort, buy the more practical kind; and six more glasses with the settings we have seen—but they must be very well packed."[13]

We have no evidence that Marx succeeded in that assignment, but his stellar performance as Seminary librarian is well documented. At the end of his first year, the library contained the most comprehensive collection of Hebrew literature in the West-

ern Hemisphere. Reporting to the board of directors on the year
from September 1903 to September 1904, Schechter noted that
of the approximately 102 Hebrew books published before the
year 1500 (known as incunabula), the Seminary library pos-
sessed 46, surpassed only by the library of the British Museum,
the Bodleian Library of Oxford, and the venerable communal
libraries of Parma (Italy) and the Jewish community of Frankfurt
(Germany).

But Marx's first year was as difficult as it was successful. He
carried a considerable teaching load, teaching at first in German
as he was not yet in full command of English. He had agreed to
devote five hours daily to the library, but this was hardly enough
time to cope with all the books and manuscripts pouring in. He
threw himself so deeply into his work that he failed to attend to
simple but expected courtesies. Thus we find a letter written in
German by Jacob Schiff, the Seminary's great patron, on November 29, 1903, in which he tartly remarks, "I had hoped that
you would pay me a visit without being specially asked." Then
Schiff continues: "Professor Friedlaender has promised to come
next Saturday for supper (7 o'clock) and to accompany us
afterwards to the theater. Won't you also give us this pleasure?"[14]

On February 5, 1904, Marx wrote a long letter, also in
German, to "Herr Judge," that is, Judge Sulzberger. He acknowledged that his work had been moving very slowly, as he
had to organize books without any assistance during the previous
six weeks. Professor Ginzberg, he continued, had recommended
a man who had previously worked in the Astor Library, and he
was hopeful that he could engage him. He also mentioned his
predicament in having to decide whether or not to buy books
offered him by bookdealers before having a reliable list of
present holdings in hand.

Schechter understood the many obstacles in Marx's way and
submitted a highly laudatory report to the board of directors:

> The reception and arrangement of so large a body of books and
> manuscripts, many of which require special bibliographical knowl-
> edge for cataloging and classifying, is an extremely difficult task. In
> spite of his professorial duties, Doctor Marx has applied himself with

a great deal of energy, zeal and intelligence in this task. The library is already in fair shape, in spite of the fact that the assistance it was possible to give him was not always of the kind that he should have had. I feel that it is due to Dr. Marx that I should make this special acknowledgment of his services to the Board.[15]

In turn, the board showed its appreciation by fixing the salary of Marx (who was still single) at $3,000 a year, commencing October 1, 1904. This compared favorably with President Schechter's starting salary of $5,000 (with annual increases) and that of Israel Davidson, appointed a year later as an instructor, at an annual salary of $1,000.[16]

But even more encouraging than the salary must have been Sulzberger's letter of October 29, 1905, giving Marx *carte blanche* in the matter of library acquisitions. "You are to appropriate the money for the purchase of such gems as you wish," he wrote, underscoring the last three words twice. "The only word I have to say is a word of advice: Do not spend all your money in one day or you will have many days of regrets. However you are the final judge of the whole matter, and so far as I am concerned, you must please yourself."[17]

A WINNING RECORD

Armed with this authority, Marx was able to claim several major collections on behalf of the Seminary. The acquisition of the library of his teacher, Moritz Steinschneider, may have been the most gratifying for him personally. In 1907, at almost 91 years of age, Steinschneider passed away in Berlin. His death enabled the Seminary to take possession of his library as a result of an unusual arrangement engineered by a former Steinschneider student, a son of an early Conservative leader, George Alexander Kohut (1874–1933).[18]

Steinschneider had never received a position commensurate with his accomplishments and capable of providing him with a decent income. In his earlier years, he had eked out a living by giving private lessons; later he became director of a girls' school and a lecturer at a small academy. Late in life, he received the title of professor from the Prussian govenment and honorary degrees from Columbia College, New York, and Hebrew Union College, Cincinnati. When Kohut, who had studied under him while a student at the *Hochschule* in Berlin, saw his old teacher again in June 1898, he was taken aback by Steinschneider's financial straits. He tactfully suggested to Steinschneider that a fund be organized toward his support, to which his many students could make contributions. Proud and independent, Steinschneider said no. Upon his return to New York, Kohut discussed the dilemma with Abraham Freidus (1867–1923), librarian of the Public Library's Jewish Division, a fine bibliographer in his own right, and a great admirer of Steinschneider. Freidus came up with the idea of selling Steinschneider's library then, with the proviso that he would retain his books during his lifetime. Excited by this solution, Kohut approached his friend Jacob Schiff. Schiff favored the idea, so Kohut entered into the delicate negotiations with Steinschneider.

On December 5, 1898, Schiff was very pleased to write to Kohut that he had received a very cordial letter from Steinschneider in which he accepted the 10,000 marks offered as the purchase price of the library. Schiff added: "I shall only hope that Prof. Steinschneider will remain for a long time yet in good health, and consequently in possession of his library, so that the question of ultimate disposal shall be far off yet."[19]

At the time of the purchase, Schiff did not assume that the Seminary would be the ultimate recipient. Instead, he wrote about the possibility of giving the "Steinschneider collection" to the New York Public Library, Columbia University, or Harvard University.[20] But by 1907, Schiff, as we have seen, had developed a keen interest in the Seminary and become its principal supporter. He was aware that Schechter, Marx, and Kohut had been students of Steinschneider, and were continuing his work in America. He knew as well of Marx's plan to edit, with Professor Henry Malter (1864–1925) of Hebrew Union College and Dropsie College, the collected works of Steinschneider. In fact, Schiff had contributed $500 to cover the cost of the first two volumes, to be published in honor of Steinschneider's ninetieth birthday on March 30, 1906.[21] In the end, it seemed most fitting to Schiff that Marx become the guardian of Steinschneider's writings, to which he himself had contributed.[22]

Another valuable collection from Germany, that of Professor Emil Friedrich Kautzsch (1841–1910), arrived at the Seminary in 1911, also through the generosity of Jacob Schiff. The collection consisted of 4,600 books and pamphlets dealing primarily with the Bible and Semitic philology, the field in which this Christian scholar had made his name. Commenting on the importance of the acquisition, Marx said, "It practically created that department in the library."[23]

For Schechter, this acquisition was an important source for his teaching programs. In his first public address before the Judean Literary Circle, on May 29, 1902, Schechter stated that the first order of business for Jewish scholars was to reclaim the Bible.[24] For the Jewish Bible (in Christian terminology, the Old Testament) had become the domain of those university professors who held that "the Old Testament and the whole history of Israel were a mere preamble to the history of Christianity." These professors, whose most prominent representative was Julius Wellhausen (1844–1918), developed the school of "higher criticism," which held that the Bible was the product of several component elements.

Schechter, not opposed to criticism, wrote:

> Criticism is nothing more than the expression of conscience on the part of the student . . . The attempt at an analysis of the Bible into component elements, whether one agrees with its results or assumes a skeptical attitude towards them, is one of the finest intellectual feats of this century; though a good deal of brutal vivisection is daily done by restless spirits whose sole ambition is to outdo their masters. . . . But, as someone has remarked, if tradition is not infallible, neither are any of its critics.[25]

But over the years, Schechter came to question the motives of those German professors, ultimately prompting his famous equation, "Higher Criticism–Higher Anti-Semitism." Remembering the physical pain of the beatings he had suffered as a child in his native Rumania, Schechter drew a parallel to the suffering he experienced after emigrating to the "civilized" countries, where "Higher Anti-Semitism started at the same time as the so-called Higher Criticism of the Bible." Taking Wellhausen as a typical example, Schechter derided his writings as "teeming with venom against Judaism, and you cannot wonder that he was rewarded by one of the highest Orders which the Prussian Government had to bestow." And further:

> This intellectual persecution can only be fought by intellectual weapons and unless we make an effort to recover our Bible and to think out our theology for ourselves, we are irrevocably lost from both worlds. . . . Our great claim to the gratitude of mankind is that we gave to the world the word of God, the Bible.[26]

Characteristically, Schechter uttered these strong words at a banquet in honor of Dr. Kaufmann Kohler, who was leaving New York to assume the presidency of Hebrew Union College in Cincinnati, the center of Reform Judaism, which has been influenced heavily by the German critical school. Despite their differences, Schechter knew Kohler well and respected him for his intellectual honesty. Moreover, Schechter never liked the term "Reform," which, in his words, "savors of schism." Tirelessly and with some success, he tried to enlist Reform rabbis in the battle for the reclamation of the Bible and other common causes. For years, Schechter served with Reform rabbis on an editorial board organized to prepare a translation of the Bible under the auspices of the Jewish Publication Society.

At the same time, Schechter was well aware that many alumni of the Hebrew Union College were dissatisfied with Kohler's leadership, and looked to him to set the direction of Judaism in America.[27] Privately, he expressed bitterness about the missionary zeal of some Hebrew Union College graduates. As he wrote to Judge Sulzberger:

> They do terrible mischief downtown. You know how much they care for Judaism, but their great aim [is] to smuggle in the Mission Prayer book[28] and other hellish things among the Russian and Roumanian Jews. Their methods are just as dishonest, dirty and

aggressive as those of the Christian missionaries. I think that we ought to make a stand against them. It is simply a farce to think that people whose whole Judaism consists in coming with their automobiles to listen to opera singers every Friday evening should now arrogate to themselves the calling of proselytysers.[29]

In the winter of 1911, Schechter went to the spa of Wiesbaden, Germany, for treatment of his failing health, and while there picked up a worrisome rumor relating to Alexander Marx and the Hildesheimer Rabbinical Seminary, where Marx's father-in-law was rector. Dr. Hirsch Hildesheimer (1885–1910), who had taught Jewish history at his father's institution in Berlin, had passed away, and Dr. Abraham Berliner (1883–1915), professor of history and literature there for many years, was due to retire. As Schechter wrote to Sulzberger:

> There is now a rumor that the two chairs will be combined into one and offered to Dr. Marx of our Seminary. What could be done if a call should be extended to Marx. I would consider Marx leaving the Seminary a terrible calamity, both to students and even more to the Library. I cannot think of the Library deprived of Marx's services. I think your feelings about the matter are fairly the same as mine, and therefore I thought that it is important that you should hear of their base intentions here and watch the developments. We must not lose Marx.[30]

Fortunately for the Seminary, Marx was not tempted to Berlin and, for the rest of his life, continued to build the library.

Even under Marx's assiduous stewardship, the library occasionally lost an exceptional opportunity to add to its holdings. A few days after warning Sulzberger about the possibility of losing Marx, Schechter again wrote informing Sulzberger that the renowned library of Baron David Guenzburg (1857–1910) of St. Petersburg, Russia, was available. A member of an affluent banking family and a scholar of Oriental languages, Guenzburg had accumulated a fine collection of rare books and 900 manuscripts. Following correspondence among Schiff, Marx, and Friedlaender, and upon the strong recommendation of Schechter, Schiff agreed to purchase this collection for the Seminary.

However, the outbreak of World War I in 1914 prevented this purchase agreement from consummation.[31] The library was later purchased for the Hebrew National Library in Jerusalem, but here, too, shipment was prevented due to the war and the Bolshevik Revolution.

Even without this addition, the library's growth was phenomenal. Thanks to the leadership of Schechter, the support of patrons Adler, Marshall, Schiff, and Sulzberger, and the diligent librarianship of Marx, the library grew from 5,000 books and only 3 manuscripts in 1903 to 43,000 volumes and 1,700 manuscripts in 1913.

SCHECHTER'S LEGACY

Schechter's success in leading the Seminary—and its library—to such distinction was due in part to his commitment to the unity of the Jewish people. He consistently made overtures to Jews of a somewhat different persuasion: Samuel Schulman (1864–1955), a Reform rabbi he recommended for an honorary Doctor of Divinity degree; Kaufmann Kohler, who, like Schulman, was invited to lecture at the Seminary; and most notably, Jacob Schiff.

Schiff shared Schechter's ecumenical views. After a convention of the Union of American Hebrew Congregations, Schiff wrote to Schechter expressing his delight

> over the spirit of good will towards the different views which was developed throughout and, as you know, this is what I have always been striving for. For, if we as Jews are to be respected in American surroundings, the prima facie condition is that we drop petty quarrels and divisions among ourselves; but rather have "malice towards none and charity for all."[32]

On other issues, consensus within the Seminary leadership was not so easily achieved. The Schechter era coincided with the rise of Zionism, which, as an idea and political movement, was repudiated by most Reform leaders of the time. Kaufmann Kohler, for example, called Zionism "a Fraud." The Reform concept of Judaism as a universal religion conflicted with the idea of a Return to Zion. Moreover, Reform leaders feared that the establishment of a Jewish state would jeopardize the political rights of Jews in their lands of residence, whether Germany or the United States. The Reform movement remained officially anti-Zionist until the Columbus Platform adopted a change in 1937.

With many of the leading Seminary backers belonging to Reform congregations, it would perhaps have been more politic for Schechter to keep silent on this issue. However, it is to the credit of Schechter that he spoke out, and to Schiff and Marshall that they continued their backing.

In expressing support for Zionism, Schechter claimed to speak as a private citizen and not as the President of the Seminary.[33] He saw Zionism as a bulwark against assimilation, and thus as the best guarantee for the preservation of Jewish identity. Because he deplored the general Zionist view of religion as a "negligible quantity," Schechter hoped that Zionism would "recreate Jewish consciousness" before creating a Jewish state.

Disharmony also characterized Schechter's relations with Schiff and others over the policies of the Educational Alliance. This agency was created by German Jews, including Schiff, to Americanize the Jewish immigrants on the East Side of New York, and Schechter served as one of its directors for many years. He agreed with the need to teach the newcomers English and prepare them for citizenship, but he held that these educational objectives should not be accomplished at the expense of courses in Hebrew language and religion. In the end he resigned, stating,

> The great question before the Jewish community at present is not so much the Americanizing of the Russian Jew as his Judaizing. We have now quite sufficient agencies for his Americanization. But the problem is whether we are able to keep the immigrant within Judaism after he has become Americanized.[34]

His desire to promote Hebrew contributed to his negative attitude toward the Yiddish language, which increased his alienation from the Yiddish-speaking masses he was so anxious to reach. The child of a Yiddish-speaking environment, he himself never used Yiddish in his own writings, but wrote in the most polished English and Hebrew. In his personal correspondence, he tended to use German. Schechter viewed Yiddish as "a mere accident in our history, doomed to die, and is dying before our very eyes. We cannot, we dare not endanger the Judaism of our children by making a virtue of what may once have been an unfortunate necessity."[35]

As the years passed, Schechter felt increasingly disillusioned about the possibility of reaching the goal of creating a theological center for all.[36] In 1905, Cyrus Adler relinquished his position as president of the board of directors and, in 1909, became head of the newly formed Dropsie College in Philadelphia. Schechter hoped that the two institutions could be merged to form one center for Jewish *Wissenschaft*, but legal considerations made such a merger impossible. In another disappointment, the new Teachers' Institute, established in 1909 with the help of a large donation from Schiff, came to be located "uptown." Schechter felt strongly that a "downtown" location, nearer the center of dense Jewish settlement, was preferable.

Schechter also became the target of attacks from the right and the left. The prime antagonist on the right was Rabbi Bernard Levinthal (1865–1952). Schechter mentions him scathingly in a letter to Sulzberger about compiling a prayerbook.

> We could, with little difficulty, compile a Prayer Book placed entirely on Talmudic and Gaonic authority, which would prove acceptable to the communities and form an antidote to the abomination they call the Hebrew Union Prayer Book. . . . The only question is whether the Orthodox Rabbis (such as Levinthal and his species, who justify their existence only by the opposition to the Seminary) could be won over to give their approval to such a Prayer Book. What I fear is that they would at once array themselves against us and dub us Reformers and Innovators, which would inflict much injury upon the Seminary.[37]

On the left was Kaufmann Kohler, president of the Hebrew Union College, who accused Schechter of expecting to lead the Jewish community by merely "consulting old manuscripts."[38]

When Schechter concluded that, to preserve the Seminary's brand of traditional Judaism, a grass-roots organization to funnel public support to the Seminary and its graduates should be created, he collided with Cyrus Adler, his long-time colleague. Adler disapproved in principle of what was to become the United Synagogue of America, arguing that it would foster divisiveness within Judaism and encourage unnecessary attacks upon Orthodoxy and Reform.[39] Schechter, who became the new organization's president on February 23, 1913, responded:

> Close observation for ten years and more has convinced me that, unless we succeed in effecting an organization, which loyal to the Torah, to the teachings of our Sages, to the tradition of our Fathers, to the usages and customs of Israel, shall at the same time introduce the English sermon and adopt scientific methods in our seminaries, on our training of Rabbis and schoolmasters for our synagogues and Talmud Torahs, and bring order and decorum in our synagogues, unless this is done, I declare unhesitatingly that Traditional Judaism will not survive another generation in this country.[40]

Even Schechter's friendship with Alexander Marx was marred by an occasional but serious disagreement. Schechter's biographer, Norman Bentwich, reports that at the outbreak of World War I they stopped walking with each other for a while. The German-born Marx sympathized with the Germans, whereas Schechter favored the Allied cause. While they resumed their walks, they agreed not to discuss the war. The story goes on: "But when they came to a newspaper stand, and there was a placard of a German success, he [Schechter] burst out: 'This paper is a damned liar.' Seeing news of an Allied success, he added: 'But lies are on the right side.' "[41]

Despite the controversies and disappointments, Schechter's accomplishments were awesome. In a relatively few short years, he raised the standards of scholarship and rabbinic training in America. Speaking at commencement on June 8, 1913, Schechter outlined his priorities for the future. He urged greater public support for the goals of the Seminary.[42] He pressed for his view that rabbis should also be scholars, and asked for additional fellowships for original research. He deplored a philanthropic system that channeled far more dollars to charitable organizations than to educational institutions. On a positive note, he thanked those who had helped make the Seminary library one of the greatest Hebrew libraries in the world. When Schechter died on November 19,1915, he left behind a foundation strong enough to support the Seminary he envisioned.

Chapter Three

The Cyrus Adler Era: 1915–1940

When Solomon Schechter died in 1915, no single individual stood out as the obvious choice to succeed him. The board of directors considered at least three faculty members to be excellent candidates for the post of president of the faculty: Louis Ginzberg, professor of Talmud, who had mentioned to his fiancée as early as 1908 that Schechter wanted him to be his successor;[1] Israel Friedlaender, professor of Bible, who had served as acting president in 1910 while Schechter was on sabbatical;[2] and Mordecai Kaplan, professor of homiletics at the Seminary and principal of the Teachers Institute, who was himself a graduate of the Seminary.

To gain time, the directors decided to make an interim appointment, and asked Cyrus Adler to become acting president. All involved thought this temporary situation would last about six months—months that stretched into years until, in 1924, the temporary appointment was recognized as permanent and "acting" was dropped from Adler's title.

The directors knew, of course, that Adler was neither a Hebrew scholar nor a rabbi, but they valued highly his assets as an excellent organizer who was deeply involved in community affairs and enjoyed ready access to the financial backers of the institution. For his part, Adler accepted the position despite his myriad other obligations—as the president of Dropsie College, as the busy editor of the *Jewish Quarterly Review*, and as the founder or director of many other educational and civic associations, Jewish and non-Jewish. Years later, he underrated his special assets when he suggested that he had been chosen president of the Seminary because he was American-born.[3]

When the board of directors named Adler acting president, it also made generous provisions for Mathilde Schechter. Originally, the contract had called for a one-time gratuity of $10,000; in addition, however, the directors voted for a lifetime pension of $3,500 a year.[4]

GAINS UNDER ADLER

The appointment of Adler would affect the Seminary for the next twenty-five years, but would not change the course of the library. Like Schechter before him, Adler appreciated the library's importance. Furthermore, Alexander Marx continued at its helm throughout Adler's term and beyond. And early supporters remained involved: for example, Judge Sulzberger, a friend of Marx and the library, added to the library's collection as long as he lived. The Schechter family, too, remained close to the library, donating 1,500 books, 1,300 manuscripts, and several Genizah fragments.

As a tribute to Solomon Schechter, Marx outlined a plan for publishing a volume of Genizah fragments. Schechter had selected between two and four hundred fragments from those offered on loan by the Cambridge library authorities in grateful recognition of his efforts in bringing many thousands of fragments from Cairo. During the last two years of his life, Schechter had been busy copying them, with a view towards publication. In fact, he had already started negotiations with a German printer in Leipzig, but the outbreak of World War I brought them to a halt. Marx recommended that these texts be distributed to the scholars on the faculty for editing: Ginzberg would be responsible for Talmudic texts, Davidson for medieval poetry, Friedlaender for Bible, and Marx himself would deal with historical texts.

Marx's proposal was too ambitious to be carried out simply

and expeditiously. Ginzberg's texts were so plentiful that they filled two volumes, requiring over ten years to publish.[5] Davidson contributed a third volume of poetry and liturgy.[6] But a tragic accident prevented the completion of Friedlaender's work: in 1920, he traveled to Russia on a relief mission for the American Joint Distribution Committee and there was murdered by bandits. His death was not only a blow to the Seminary but to the whole community which he had served as a teacher. A confirmed Zionist, he was very involved with the educational needs of the immigrants and was the chairman of the Bureau of Jewish Education in New York.[7]

In that same year, the Seminary suffered another grievous loss in the death of Jacob Schiff. It was the support of Schiff—as the principal contributor to the Seminary's budget and as an example to others—that had made possible the reorganization of the Seminary in 1902, and the start of new leadership under Schechter.

The loss of Jacob Schiff was mitigated somewhat by his son's commitment to continue his father's work. Mortimer Schiff (1877–1931) found rare books and beautiful manuscripts very alluring and, according to Marx, was always ready to authorize the purchase of books if they appealed to him.[8]

In 1921, Mortimer Schiff made possible the acquisition of 1,100 prints, and some 1,800 books and pamphlets gathered over thirty years by the British collector Israel Solomons. This acquisition made the library prominent in the field of Anglo-Jewish history.

An even more valuable treasure from England, the Elkan Nathan Adler collection, came to New York two years later. A native of London, Elkan Adler (1861–1946) was descended from a long line of rabbis. Both his father, Nathan, and his brother Hermann had served as chief rabbi of England. Adler, though, became a lawyer. In that capacity, he traveled throughout the world, visiting Morocco, Algiers, Tunis, Tripoli, Egypt, Palestine, Syria, Central Asia, Russia, and the United States. Wherever he went, he made contacts in the Jewish community and with bookdealers as he sought rare Hebrew books and manuscripts. In this way, in about thirty-five years, he gathered over 4,000 manuscripts and about 30,000 volumes. Among the items were many fragments from the Cairo Genizah which he obtained on his trip to Egypt in 1896.[9] Adding to the renown of Adler's treasures were the scholarly books and articles he published, including a catalog with over 100 facsimilies of his most interesting manuscripts.[10]

In the book world, word spread that Adler wanted to sell his library. Marx hoped to open negotiations during a trip to Europe in 1919. But Cyrus Adler dissuaded him, feeling that it was not the right moment to approach Jacob Schiff, whose financial support was necessary, to consider the matter.[11] For no matter how valuable the collection was, the aftermath of World War I had created more urgent needs for American Jewish philanthropists.

But the opportunity was too precious to ignore for long. In a lengthy letter dated November 8, 1922—two years after Jacob Schiff's death—Cyrus Adler tried to impress Schiff's son Mortimer with the importance of the Adler collection. He compared it with the famous David Oppenheimer (1664–1736) collection, which had been purchased in 1829 by the Bodleian Library in England, thus making that library the foremost center of Hebrew books.[12] Included in his letter was a memorandum from Marx which described the Adler holdings in detail and stated that their acquisition would make the Seminary the world's largest collection of Hebrew books and manuscripts. In support of Marx, Adler quoted Dr. Abraham Rosenbach (1876–1952), the well-known rare book dealer from Philadelphia. This expert had examined the library three times and stated that it filled seven large rooms in Elkan Adler's home. Rosenbach also quoted an asking price of 30,000 pounds given him by the owner, but he added that he felt a counteroffer of 22,500 pounds would be acceptable.[13]

Pressure was mounting, since Hebrew Union College, through its librarian, Adolph S. Oko (1885–1944), was also interested in acquiring the Adler Collection. In 1922, on a trip to Europe, Oko had been told that the price was $120,000, and at that time his board of governors felt that a new dormitory was a more pressing need.[14] Oko continued with his efforts nonetheless, but gave up when told by Marx early in 1923 that the Seminary was in the field.[15]

On February 6, 1923, Cyrus Adler had in hand a list of subscribers who had pledged $100,000. At the top of the list was Mortimer Schiff with $50,000, Felix Warburg, his brother-in-law, with $10,000, and Louis Marshall with $10,000.[16] On March 15, Rosenbach cabled that Adler's final price was 25,000 pounds or $105,000. This price included all of Adler's Judaica collection, both manuscripts and printed books, with the stipulation that all duplicates would be returned to Adler's estate after the Seminary chose the copies it wanted.

On March 19, Cyrus Adler announced to the press that the addition of the Elkan Adler collection made the Seminary the owner of the greatest Jewish library in the world. His announcement listed the names of other subscribers, including Nathan Miller, Henry S. Hendricks, Jules Mastbaum, Daniel Guggenheim, Felix Fuld, Sol, Louis S., and Joseph Stroock, Herbert Lehman, and Jacob Epstein.

As fate would have it, the first shipment of sixty-four cases arrived on April 17, 1923, three days before the death of Judge Sulzberger, whose earlier gifts had established the library's prominence. Moreover, his will left a $10,000 bequest to the Seminary and mandated that his remaining books be divided between the Seminary, Dropsie College, and Gratz College, with Cyrus Adler as the executor.[17]

THE LIBRARY INCORPORATES
Marx was now in charge of 80,000 volumes and 6,000 manuscripts. In addition to increasing the quality of the library's holdings, the Adler Collection allowed Marx to complement editions in which some of the pages were missing. With his eminent knowledge of paleography, he could match loose leaves acquired on previous occasions with leaves and fragments found in Adler's collection.

Marx's satisfaction would have been even greater had he been given a larger staff with increased remuneration for the difficult work of cataloging. From the Seminary *Registers*, it is evident that for many years Marx had only one ranking assistant, Israel Shapira, listed as a cataloger. When in 1916 Marx asked for the appointment of an assistant librarian and a raise in salary for Phillip Abrahams, the library's assistant, he was turned down for lack of funds.[18] However, in 1923, the staffing picture improved somewhat, due in part to the work generated by the large Adler Collection. The names of two new catalogers, Joshua Finkel and Isaac Rivkind, appear in subsequent *Registers*.

We know little about Finkel, but quite a bit about Rivkind. Born in 1898 in Lodz, Poland, he had studied at the famous Lithuanian yeshivot of Volozhin and Poniewicz. He arrived in the United States in 1920, and became active in the religious Zionist movement. In 1923, he was employed as an assistant in the library for a monthly salary of $125. His fine Hebrew background made him a very valuable employee, so Marx pleaded with the trustees to raise Rivkind's salary to the same level as Finkel's: $200 a month. When the board failed to act on his request, Marx sent an urgent appeal to Mortimer Schiff, asking him to make up the difference.[19] Three years later, when Rivkind married, Marx pleaded again for a raise to $235 a month, which was granted. Rivkind would remain with the library for thirty-five years, retiring as chief of the Hebraic section with many scholarly achievements. An indebted Seminary awarded him an honorary doctorate in 1952, and retired him with full pay in 1959.

In 1924, the library was incorporated. As the *Register* noted at the time: "The Library of the Seminary having grown in magnitude, and in addition to serving the Faculty and students of the Seminary having become of importance for scholars throughout the world, the Directors of the Seminary deemed it advisable to establish a separate corporation for its management."[20]

The incorporation was intended in part to broaden the library's base of financial support. The expense of acquiring the Elkan Adler collection had put a heavy burden on a handful of contributors, particularly Mortimer Schiff, the library's princi-

pal patron after the death of his father. Schiff felt that by making
the library a legally separate unit, able to receive donations
independently of the Seminary, a greater circle of supporters
could be developed. For while people might disagree with the
philosophy of Judaism as taught and preached at the Seminary
and not want to support it, few would make a case against the
support of an excellent library open to all.

The library's new status boosted the standing of Marx's staff.
The *Register* of 1925 lists three new names, including the assist-
ant librarian for whom Marx had been lobbying for so long.
That post was filled by Rabbi Benjamin (later listed as Boaz)
Cohen (1899–1968), a 1924 Seminary graduate. At the same
time Cohen was named to the faculty as an instructor of Talmud.
This assured him faculty status, which the position of a librarian
alone did not carry. In both teaching and librarianship, Cohen
distinguished himself. His scholarly works include *Kunteres ha
Teshuvot*, an annotated bibliography of Rabbinic responsa; *Law
and Tradition in Judaism: Jewish and Roman Law* (2 vols.); and
bibliographies on Israel Friedlaender, Louis Ginzberg, and Alexander Marx.

The second newcomer, Dr. Saul Gittelsohn, carried the title
"cataloger," and appears as such until 1937. The third addition
was Anna Kleban, secretary to the librarian. A niece of Professor Israel Davidson, Kleban would be associated with the library
for more than half a century. One of her favorite duties was
introducing the Seminary's many visitors to the treasures of the
Rare Book Room, which she did with great charm and wit until
advancing years forced her retirement in 1982.

The expansion of the library testifies to Marx's talents as a
librarian, but he influenced generations of students as a teacher
and a scholar as well. In 1928, the year he turned fifty, Marx
could look back on twenty-five years of service as professor of
history and head of the largest collection of Hebrew books and
manuscripts in the Western world. In honor of Marx's birthday,
Boaz Cohen prepared an essay and bibliography on his work.[21]
The bibliography lists 186 items. Most appreciated in its day
was the one-volume *History of the Jewish People* (1927), authored

jointly by Marx and Professor Max L. Margolis (1866–1932) of
Dropsie College. The book is comprehensive, concentrated, and
factual, serving as a reference volume on Jewish history. By 1945
it had appeared in seven printings.

Over the years, Marx was consulted by countless correspon-
dents on texts and manuscripts which, thanks to the Seminary's
large holdings, he was able to furnish. He also influenced
Seminary graduates to continue their scholarly research after
entering the active rabbinate. Below, in its entirety, is a letter
written to him by the gifted graduate Milton Steinberg (1903–
1950), after his first two years as a rabbi in Indianapolis.

I presume that hearing from me is very much like receiving a
spiritualistic message from the dead. I can imagine the shock and
surprise that a letter like this must entail, and yet, through all my
silence, I have often thought of you and your family and what they
have meant in the past and still mean. I am writing this letter in the
hope that I have not fallen so far from grace as not to merit a reply.

My work in Indianapolis is still very interesting and still rewarded
by some measure of success. My congregation has grown considera-
bly in size and while, of course, we have budget problems (we would
not be a Jewish congregation if we did not) we are permanently
established as a real force in the community. My two years of
experience in the active ministry have taught me the meaning of that
phrase that one hears Rabbis employ so generally "too busy to do
scholarly work." I have resisted as much as I could the absorption of
all my time in congregational activities and I try to keep free time for
study and reading.

I read Midrash and Mishna religiously and, on the average, one
good book a week, but I am overcome by a sense of futility and
frustration. My reading seems to be getting nowhere; it is too
diffuse, scattered and unorganized. That is why I am writing to you.

There are two things that I want you to help me on if you can and
will. One is this,—ever since I reported on IV Ezra I have felt that
there was room for a popular presentation of that very remarkable
challenge to the Theodicy. I have long wanted to write a literary
essay on that book. To the best of my knowledge, however, there is
not a single copy of it in Indianapolis. Do you know where I can buy
a copy? I have tried all the stores in New York. Or perhaps do you
know of a copy that I can borrow for a month or so. I think that it is a
shame that so fine a literary work should be denied any popular

exposition. If, therefore, you can get a hold of a copy for me, I shall
be much indebted to you. I shall, of course, be happy to meet any
expenses involved.

In addition to this one project which I am contemplating, I am
sure that you can be of service to me in another respect. There must
be some problem you would like to have worked out, some matter of
research, no matter how painstaking and minute. Can't you let me
try my hand at it. You must remember, of course, that if the
problem is such that it involves the use of obscure books, that I will
have to get the facilities and the tools from outside of Indianapolis.

I have a sincere sense of guilt when I write to a man as busy as you
are, posing questions and asking for help. I suppose that it is pure
presumption on my part and yet you told us time and again that you
wanted to hear from us after we left the seminary and that you
would be glad to encourage, in engaging in research. It is that fact
that gives me the courage to make so unusual a request. I hope that
you will find time to give to an obscure Rabbi engaged in attempting
to keep Judaism alive in a completely de-judaized obscure town.

Please convey my warmest personal respect to Mrs. Marx, to the
children, and to Henry.

Cordially,
Milton Steinberg

[*Written by hand*]
P.S. Why is it that dictated letters always sound so fearfully
impersonal? A stenographer seems a blessing in disguise but in
actuality proves a positive menace to spontaneity so that if this letter
seems to be a monument to imperialism—you'll take my word for it
that it is the fault of the Gregg method and the typewriter.

M.S.[22]

A BUILDING PROGRAM
Overcrowding was about to overcome the Seminary and the
library. As early as 1923, Marx had envisioned a 200,000-volume
library, and Adler, as the Seminary's chief administrator, began
to work out the details of an expansion. At first, attention
focused on two recently acquired buildings adjoining the now-
bulging 123rd Street facility, with the idea of converting them
into a library. As if foreseeing the conflagration of 1966, Adler
wrote to Mortimer Schiff about the perils of fire: "There is
always a greater danger of fire when a building does not stand

independently, because the danger comes from within as well as from one's neighbors."[23]

Ultimately a different solution to the Seminary's building needs was found. The prime mover behind the Seminary's relocation to Broadway and 122nd Street in 1929 was Louis Marshall (1856–1929), who served as chairman of the Seminary's board of directors from 1909 until his death twenty years later.

Like most of the Seminary's early supporters, he was of German-Jewish descent. Influencing him from the beginning in the direction of Jewish interest was his mother, a deeply religious woman.[24] Marshall, a native of Syracuse, entered Columbia Law School, where he completed the regular two-year curriculum in one year, and was admitted to the Bar when just twenty-one years old. Although successful and very much at home in Syracuse, he was pleased to be invited to New York City, which offered greater opportunity for a bright young lawyer. In 1894, he joined the New York firm of Guggenheimer and Untermyer, adding his own name to the firm's masthead. A year later, he married Florence, daughter of Benedict Lowenstein. It was a happy union that resulted in four children. Sadly, Mrs. Marshall died at the early age of forty-three.

Marshall's own energy never flagged. Acting at the highest level, he effected changes on the world stage on several occasions.[25] For example, in 1911, he led the fight to abrogate the Russian-American Treaty of 1832, because it discriminated against Jews holding American passports. And in 1919, he attended the Paris Peace Conference at the end of World War I, and helped secure international guarantees for the rights of minorities, irrespective of religious or national background.

Following Jacob Schiff, a close associate of his, he became involved early with the Seminary and was sympathetic to its role in the Jewish life of America. As he recounts:

> On Mr. Schiff's insistence I became the Chairman of the Executive Committee, and later Chairman of the Board of Directors, and have followed every step in the growth of the institution. The fact that I am likewise President of Temple Emanu-El and greatly interested in Hebrew Union College may, at first blush, appear to be inconsistent

with my interest in the Seminary, but my answer is and always has been, that nothing Jewish is alien to me, that there is no royal road by which alone an object can be attained, and that it is necessary to utilize every agency which will bring about the result which we are seeking to obtain, namely the perpetuation of Judaism as a living religion and as a great influence upon civilization.[26]

In a letter to a "dissatisfied student," Marshall took the trouble to expound further.

You are constantly speaking of American Judaism. You refer to its life and death struggles. You again and again mention American ministers. There is no such thing as American Judaism, as distinguished from any other species of Judaism. In the term Judaism, there is comprehended a system of beliefs, doctrine, and a view of life and of the relations of man to God, which is in principle unchanging and unchangeable. It is the same in Palestine as in New York; in Russia as in Chicago. . . . Judaism and Americanism can go hand in hand. The most orthodox, the most conservative Jew, is probably as good an American, as the so called reform Jew. . . . There is no life and death struggle of Judaism in America. . . . But its life and death are not dependent upon the question of whether or not the Seminary can satisfy each of its pupils as to each of its faculty, and as to each member of the student body. Every man is supposed to do his duty as best he may.[27]

Marshall demonstrated his respect for all things Jewish time and time again. To get close to the Yiddish-speaking masses and to assist their adjustment to America, he became a trustee of the Educational Alliance, the agency which organized the educational programs for immigrants. Historian Oscar Handlin notes: "Although the East Siders were often suspicious of him as a 'German' and 'Yehudi,' he was eager to establish contact with them. He deplored the jeers at Yiddish as an uncouth jargon; indeed he went to the trouble of learning the language to be able to meet the immigrants on their own ground."[28] President of Temple Emanu-El when that Reform congregation was embarking on the design and construction of a new building on Fifth Avenue, he wrote to Professor Louis Ginzberg, the Seminary's renowned authority on Jewish law, for his views on "the limitations upon decorations imposed by the practises of traditional Judaism. . . . It is our desire to avoid the use of any decoration which would offend the sensibilities of the most orthodox." Upon receiving Ginzberg's reply, he stated: "We shall act in strictest accord with it in the construction and decoration of the new Synagogue of Emanu-El congregation."[29]

Marshall's principal function as chairman of the Seminary board was to raise funds for the institution. In support of his solicitations, he has left us some telling observations. In 1924, he writes:

> It is a sad fact, however, which must not be overlooked, that too many of our wealthy Jews confine their philanthropic activities to hospitals, orphan-asylums, homes for the aged, and institutions of like character, and hold themselves aloof from our religious life and from the education of our youth in Judaism. That makes the conduct of such an institution as ours exceptionally difficult, and places the burden upon a small body. I think that fully one-half of all the money we have received for endowment purposes and for the construction of our buildings and the acquisition of our library and other collections, has come from Mr. Schiff, his son Mortimer, and Mr. Warburg.[30]

Modestly, Marshall omits his own name; however, the records show that he too was a substantial contributor.

One of the most philanthropic of Marshall's peers was Julius Rosenwald (1862–1932), president of Sears, Roebuck and Company, the Chicago-based mail-order house. To Marshall, Rosenwald suggested merging the Seminary and Hebrew Union College, with the understanding that Rosenwald would make a substantial long-term contribution to the consolidated corporation. In his thoughtful reply of June 27, 1921, Marshall recalled that he too, along with Judge Sulzberger, Jacob Schiff, and others, had once considered this option, but they had rejected it as neither practical nor economical. In great detail he explained to Rosenwald that the philosophies and attitudes toward tradition of the two institutions were so different that any attempt at fusion would be rejected as insincere and hypocritical.[31] Marshall, like his great friend Schechter, refused to forsake principle for expediency.

A few years later, in August of 1929, he again wrote Rosenwald. This long letter is a classic exposition of the role of the Seminary as he saw it. It was written from the ship on which he was traveling to Europe for a meeting in Zurich, Switzerland, of the Jewish Agency for Palestine, and was prompted by Felix Warburg, who had informed him that Rosenwald planned to support Yeshiva (now Yeshiva University) in its program to add secular training to the theological department.[32] Marshall himself did not view the establishment of Jewish colleges and universities with favor. He feared it might have a harmful effect on Jewish students "who desire to attend the long-established institutions of higher learning in this country," by leading to a *numerus clausus* (restricted admission of Jews), as prevailed in German, Polish, Austrian, and Hungarian universities. In arguing for support of the Seminary, Marshall referred first to unsuccessful attempts at combining Yeshiva with his own institution. He stated that "the leaders of Yeshiva were so ultra-orthodox that they imposed conditions which we were unwilling to sanction. Thus, they asked us to pledge ourselves to the propositions that if any of our graduates should serve in a Congregation which maintained family pews, or a mixed choir, or an organ we would ostracize them." He then pointed with great pride to what the Seminary had achieved on its own. It had built from scratch the greatest Jewish library in the world and the finest museum of ceremonial objects in America. And further:

> We have graduated more than two hundred rabbis, we have maintained a Teachers Institute, which has supplied competent instructors for the various religious schools of the country. Today, there are over four hundred pupils in that branch of our institution. Thanks to the generosity of the late Mr. Brush, we have received funds, which enable us to construct and maintain a dormitory for our students and a support fund for those of them who stand in need of it. The Schiff family is providing us with a building which will adequately house our literary treasures. Mr. Unterberg is erecting a structure for the

Teachers Institute. The lands and buildings referred to, with their equipment, involve a cost of nearly two million dollars. The fund is in hand and we shall not be obliged to incur any indebtedness. But the expense of operating our institutions worthily and efficiently, of paying our faculty compensations comfortable with reasonable needs, of adding strength to it, by recruiting its ranks, of stimulating growth and natural development will require a large fund. We, who have staggered for so many years under a heavy load, are getting older. We would like to feel before we pass from this earthly scene that the Seminary is provided for.[33]

On September 27, 1929, the *American Hebrew* carried the following notice: "Julius Rosenwald . . . has given $500,000.—to the Jewish Theological Seminary of America to set up an endowment to be known as the Louis Marshall Memorial Fund. . . . In making the offer, Mr. Rosenwald wrote that it had been inspired by a letter which Mr. Marshall wrote shortly before his death."[34] Thus, even after his death, Marshall served the institution that had benefited so much from his life's work. The new buildings mentioned in his letter to Rosenwald were dedicated during the week of October 19 to 26, 1930. Mortimer L. Schiff presented the keys of the library building, named the Jacob H. Schiff Memorial, to Sol M. Stroock on behalf of the Library Corporation. Addresses were delivered by Alexander Marx, A.S.W. Rosenbach, president of the American Jewish Historical Society, and William W. Rockwell, the librarian of the neighboring Union Theological Seminary.

The movement of the 79,000 books, 7,000 manuscripts, and collections of incunabula, rare books, and ceremonial objects had been completed in October 1930, and the library was opened for public use in January 1931. The building included a ten-floor tower, with the capacity to house 299,000 volumes. Space was sufficiently ample to provide facilities for the American Jewish Historical Society. Separate buildings were erected for the Teachers Institute, the Unterberg Memorial, and for students, the Louis S. Brush Memorial.

The Seminary was able to complete its ambitious building program despite the Wall Street Crash of October 1929. The economic collapse sealed off many sources of support, but luckily the major contributions, headed by the Louis S. Brush bequest of $1.5 million, had arrived prior to the Crash, allowing the builders to complete their task.

LEAN TIMES

Pinpointing the year 1931, Marx wrote, "the normal continuous development of the library came to a sudden stop and the appropriations for the purchase of books were practically cut off."[35] But funds were not the library's only resource. A steady flow of individual gifts continued, made in acknowledgment of the Seminary and its library as centers of research, and in appreciation for the assistance of Alexander Marx.

During this period, Rabbi Hyman G. Enelow (1877–1934) was a great friend of the library. Born in Kovno, Lithuania, he came to America as a youth and was ordained by the Hebrew Union College in 1898.[36] A thoughtful spokesman for Reform Judaism, rabbi of New York's Temple Emanu-El since 1912, busy with raising the level of Jewish knowledge among children and adults, he was also a fine scholar. He published two important volumes, the *Menorat Hamaor* and the *Mishnah of Rabbi Eliezer*, which brought him great acclaim in the scholarly community.[37] In his research, he was greatly assisted by Alexander Marx, and by Louis Ginzberg, to whom he dedicated his *Mishnah of Rabbi Eliezer*. His zeal for scholarship was shared by Mrs. Linda R. Miller (1877–1936), a member of his synagogue who, in 1932, donated to the library a valuable collection of 1,100 manuscripts gathered from all parts of the Orient. (After Enelow's death, she designated it the Enelow Memorial Collection.) He also influenced Mrs. Miller to establish a professorship of Jewish history, literature and institutions at Columbia University in memory of her husband, Nathan, who had been a great patron of literature and the arts. Many leading Hebrew scholars of the day honored her name by contributing articles to a memorial volume which was edited by Professor Israel Davidson and published by the Seminary, with a foreword by Cyrus Adler.[38]

When Enelow retired from Temple Emanu-El, his friends suspected that he had been forced out. Israel Davidson, Louis Ginzberg, and Alexander Marx signed a letter addressed to Judge Irving Lehman, president of the temple and a director of the Seminary, praising Enelow as a great scholar and expressing surprise at his retirement. A laudatory letter was sent as well by Saul Lieberman (1898–1983), then in charge of the Harry Fischel Institute for Talmudic Research in Jerusalem (and later professor of Talmud at the Seminary).[39] Sadly, Enelow did not see that letter, for he died February 5, 1934, on his way to Europe.

Marx credited Enelow with procuring a number of donations for the library and acknowledged with gratitude Enelow's decision to will his magnificent collection to it.[40] The collection included beautiful editions that reflected Enelow's wide range of interests in history, philosophy, theology, art, bibliography, and general literature, all bound artistically by expert bookbinders in France.

Still another of Enelow's friends, Lucius N. Littauer (1859–1944), became a great benefactor of the library at a time when the Seminary had little money for the purchase of new books. Littauer had served in the United States Congress from 1897 to 1907, and later, as a glove manufacturer, amassed a sizable fortune. A major philanthropist, he established a professorship of Jewish literature and philosophy at Harvard University. To improve its Jewish book collection, Littauer bought for Harvard the Hebraica duplicates of the Enelow collection from the Seminary, in 1937, for $10,000. The sale enabled Marx to purchase several valuable manuscripts and rare books. These additions were incorporated into the Enelow collection.

ASSISTANCE TO REFUGEE SCHOLARS

The Depression of the 1930's intensified the financial difficulties of the Seminary. But the Seminary's financial footing had never been secure. From the beginning, its budgetary requirements were met by a relatively few individuals who were financially able and saw the need for training traditionally oriented, English-speaking rabbis. The Seminary lacked a broad network of Seminary graduates and their congregations, organized to ensure the Seminary a steady stream of support. Compounding the problem was the rise of Nazi Germany, which created countless emergencies abroad, draining charitable dollars from all members of the Jewish community.

These developments converged in creating the plight of the refugee scholars. Scholars who had lost their positions in Germany were anxiously looking for help from America at a time when the poor financial situation of the Seminary limited its participation in their rescue.[41]

In several instances, though, the Seminary was able to help. In April 1934, using a grant from the Emergency Committee in Aid of Displaced German Scholars, the Seminary secured the services for one year of Dr. Alexander Sperber, a Biblical expert from the University of Bonn. This arrangement was then extended for two additional years, after which Sperber became a member of the Seminary faculty. A place was also found for Professor Julius Lewy, formerly of the University of Giessen, who taught ancient Oriental history for one semester. The Seminary participated as well in bringing Professor Ismar Elbogen (1874–1945), the noted historian, to the United States. He was given an office at the Seminary where he pursued his research and offered his assistance to other refugee scholars.

The Seminary came to the rescue of Rabbi Max Gruenewald, the spiritual leader of the Mannheim Jewish community, in a different way. He had emigrated with his family to Palestine in the fall of 1938. Early in 1939, he received an invitation from the acting president, Dr. Louis Finkelstein, to be a guest at the Seminary for one year and use that time for research, but the advent of the war left him stranded alone in New York. Gruenewald writes:

> When I returned to Palestine, Italy declared war. The boats were ordered back. Our boat which was already near Lisbon (Portugal), was returned to New York. I spent 3 weeks on Ellis Island, and I was soon after that again guest of the Seminary. Attempts to reach my wife and son in Israel failed.

From 1939 until 1944 I stayed at the Seminary, worked part time for the Cultural Department of the World Congress and for the American Friends of the Hebrew University. . . . In the year 1944, I became weekend Rabbi of Millburn, N.J. In the year 1945, I left the States, in order to rejoin my family. In the year 1946, I accepted a full time rabbinate in Millburn, from which I retired in the year 1970.[42]

Chapter Four

The Next Generation: Louis Finkelstein Becomes President

On April 7, 1940, Cyrus Adler died, and on May 1, Louis Finkelstein succeeded him as president of the Seminary. Finkelstein was the choice not only of the board of directors but also of the Seminary's rank and file. The chairman of the board, Sol M. Stroock, emphasized Finkelstein's favorite-son status in a press release announcing the appointment.

> Dr. Finkelstein was Dr. Adler's intimate friend and adviser for many years. In making this appointment, the members of the Board of Directors feel that they are acting in accordance with the desire of the alumni and faculty of the institution. We are proud to announce Doctor Finkelstein's election to the Presidency of the Seminary.[1]

Finkelstein was a product of the Seminary and, as such, ideally suited to help the Seminary flourish in a new climate. Born in Cincinnati, Ohio, on June 14, 1895, he was to earn degrees at City College and Columbia University as well as graduate, in 1919, from the Seminary's Rabbinical School. For eleven years, beginning in 1920, he served as rabbi of Congregation Kehilath Israel in New York and part-time on the Seminary faculty. In 1931, he was appointed to the Solomon Schechter Chair of Theology, and in 1937, accepted the position of provost as well.

With this background, Finkelstein was able to steer clear of the shortcomings of Adler's administration. For example, the faculty had harbored reservations about Adler's ability to be a leader of Jewish scholarship, but considered Finkelstein to be one of their own. Adler openly acknowledged this situation in a letter to Felix Warburg, dated May 19, 1924. In this letter, he recommends Louis Ginzberg for American advisor to the new Hebrew University of Jerusalem, writing:

> It would be worthwhile even to ask him [Ginzberg] to go to Europe for the purpose. I do not often make statements so definitely as this, but I am sure that what I am suggesting to you is very important. I think that Jewish scholars are getting a little tired of my ubiquitous presidency, chairmanship, etc. and I think rightly so.[2]

Adler's great strength—close contacts with affluent circles—grew less important as the needs of the Seminary changed. The new Seminary, with its greatly expanded program, needed a broader base of support. Seminary graduates, active in Conservative congregations throughout the country, were ready-made for the role, and Finkelstein was in a position to tap this critical group. His fellow graduates respected his credentials as a scholar. After his graduation from the Seminary, he continued his Talmudic studies privately under the eminent Talmudist Louis Ginzberg, who bestowed upon him the certificate of *Hattarat Horaah* (full authority on questions of religious law).

Finkelstein's early career was admired as a model of how to combine active congregational work with research, a goal of many Seminary graduates. While at Congregation Kehilath Israel, he published works which brought him wide attention in scholarly circles in the United States and abroad, leading to his being considered for a position at the renowned Rabbinical Seminary of Breslau, Germany.[3] His candidacy was supported by a letter of recommendation from Alexander Marx to Dr. Albert Lefkowitz, dated July 25, 1927, stating that Finkelstein could easily qualify for a teaching position in history, Talmud, or Jewish philosophy.[4] Marx further described him as a strict conservative, adding "perhaps orthodox," whose views were based on the concept of historical Judaism. Asked about this episode almost sixty years later, Dr. Finkelstein confided: "I am glad I didn't go. I might have perished in the Holocaust."[5]

THE SEMINARY IN TRANSITION

If Finkelstein represented the new generation, Marx, along with Ginzberg and Kaplan, constituted the Seminary's old guard. To the new president, Marx was teacher and advisor, and he respectfully consulted him about decisions affecting the academic program. In a letter dated June 25, 1941, Finkelstein informed Marx of new appointments to the faculty of the Rabbinical School.[6] The outstanding roster included Saul Lieberman, professor of Palestinian literature and institutions; H. L. Ginsberg, Sabato Morais professor of Biblical history and literature; Boaz Cohen, associate professor of rabbinics; Simon Greenberg, associate professor of education; Robert Gordis, associate professor of Biblical exegesis; Alexander Sperber, reader and research fellow in Biblical versions; and Hillel Bavli, William Prager lecturer in Hebrew literature.

With America's entry into the war, Finkelstein proposed an accelerated program of rabbinic training. This would help the Seminary provide the armed forces with more chaplains. Understanding the possible resistance of Seminary professors to condensing rabbinic training into a three-year from a four-year program, Finkelstein approached Marx for support.[7] Happily, Finkelstein's proposal was accepted, and the Seminary was able to add an extra measure to its support of the war effort.

As a senior faculty member, Marx played a considerable role in the Seminary's administration. In its internal deliberations, he was a champion of traditionalism. This position led him into conflict with Mordecai Kaplan, another venerable Seminary professor. As principal of the Teachers Institute and Seminary professor of homiletics, Kaplan exercised enormous influence over his students. His novel interpretations of Judaism, which formed the basis of the Reconstructionist movement, brought him up against the more traditional members of the faculty. The internal disagreement erupted into the open in 1945, when Kaplan published a new prayerbook. By incorporating his philosophy of Judaism, the volume made basic changes in the traditional text, provoking Marx, Ginzberg, and Lieberman to denounce the volume in a letter to the Hebrew weekly *Hadoar*.[8] If Finkelstein concurred with these three faculty members on this issue, as is generally assumed, he remained above the controversy.

Finkelstein's cordial relations with the senior faculty members were displayed at a testimonial dinner held in honor of his fiftieth birthday, June 26, 1945. In the style of such events, Ginzberg, Kaplan, and Marx praised Finkelstein, who returned their compliments most eloquently, describing the Seminary as an institution where people of different views could work together.[9] His comments about Marx, though, are especially worth repeating, for, more than a compliment, they were an appreciative appraisal of a man who had devoted over forty years to building the Seminary library. He said:

> It is a great thing to have in Professor Marx a man who is a great scholar, but is more than a great scholar. It took more than great scholarship to build up that library. It took great wisdom and penetration; some time get him to tell you the story of how he wrangled a certain library over to us. And it was no easy business. This library didn't become the greatest Jewish library in the world simply because Dr. Marx knows manuscripts, but also because he is a mighty practical person.[10]

MARX AS CURATOR

Marx turned his talents to the Seminary's collection of ceremonial objects as well. He appreciated the connection between books, as artifacts of Jewish learning, and ceremonial objects, as artifacts of Jewish practice.

The collection began with the treasures of the Benguiat acquisition. In 1925, Felix M. Warburg bought it on the recommendation of Cyrus Adler, and donated it to the Seminary. First housed in the 123rd Street building, the objects made the move to the Seminary's new quarters, at which point they were presented as the Seminary museum and opened to the public on November 23, 1931.[11] The museum's holdings grew year by year, and its exhibits attracted ever-larger numbers of visitors. In a letter drafted for circulation among Seminary-affiliated rabbis, Marx reported that 26,000 visitors came to the museum in 1941.[12]

In a now familiar pattern, growth meant the need for more space. Felix Warburg's widow, Frieda (1876–1958), agreed to donate to the museum her family's former residence at 1109 Fifth Avenue. The transfer was to take place on January 14, 1944, the seventy-third anniversary of her late husband's birth. The new museum building was opened to the public on May 7, 1947.

The Seminary library and museum, under Marx, became important repositories of the European Jewish heritage. In what was, tragically, a unique case, the Jewish community of Danzig shipped its ceremonial objects to the Seminary for safekeeping until the time when the Nazi fury would pass. This collection was destined to become a sacred memorial to a once-flourishing Jewish community.

In other cases, what was salvaged of European Jewish life were mere pieces, picked up and put together with extraordinary devotion by American military personnel and civilians after the war. When the Allied armies entered Germany during World War II, they found approximately eight million foreign nationals, most of whom had been brought in by the Germans to work for the Nazi war machine. One of the difficult tasks confronting the military was the repatriation of these displaced persons to their former homelands.

Also stranded in Germany were approximately 50,000 Jews, survivors of the camps. Repatriation was not an option for the surviving Jews, who did not have a homeland. They were forced to remain in and around the displaced-persons camps, in Germany, until havens became available in the new State of Israel and elsewhere.[13]

The Allied armies also had to contend with millions of books and cultural objects that had survived the war. Some of these items were identifiably German and had been placed in storage by the Nazis in order to protect them from aerial bombardment.

But tens of thousands of these objects were treasures that the Nazis had looted from the Jewish communities and Jewish individuals they had destroyed.

A commission on European Jewish Cultural Reconstruction, headed by Professor Salo W. Baron of Columbia University, had been formed in part to deal with the reclamation of this property. While the full fury of the Holocaust did not become known to the world until after the war, enough information had become available before 1945 to anticipate the wholesale destruction of Jewish life in Europe, and the commission's goal was to look ahead to the task of rebuilding the shattered communities. Its work would include a survey of the Jewish scene as it existed prior to the war and advising the United Nations on the reconstruction of the cultural aspects of Jewish life.[14] The commission had the full support of leading Jewish organizations, such as the American Joint Distribution Committee, the American Jewish Committee, and the American Association for Jewish Education, and enjoyed the expertise of many scholars and educators who had themselves escaped from Nazi Europe. Alexander Marx was an active member of the commission. He headed the subcommittee on research, which submitted a detailed survey of the educational institutions in Europe before the rise of the Nazis.

In the fall of 1945, Professor Baron and members of the commission met with General Lucius D. Clay (1897–1978), the officer responsible for civil affairs in the U.S. Zone of Germany. They advised him to set up a special depot to serve as a collection point for the millions of books and cultural objects found by the military. From this central point, efforts to return all captured materials to their legitimate owners could commence. As a result of this meeting, the Offenbach depot was established, and for three crucial years, from 1946 to 1949, it served as the hub for receiving, sorting, and shipping over three million items.

The first director of the depot was Captain Seymour J. Pomrenze, an experienced archivist and linguist. He had been serving as the archivist of Wuerttemberg-Baden, but was reassigned to his new post on the recommendation of Judge Simon

H. Rifkind, the civilian advisor on Jewish affairs from October 1945 to March 1946. Although on the job for only six weeks, Pomrenze made contacts with the liaison officers from the countries that had properties at the depot, and established the ground rules for the depot's operations. Understanding the enormity of the task, he increased the personnel from 6 to 176. The staff handled those items whose actual owners could be traced with relative dispatch. But with Jewish books and cultural items, the owners were most likely dead and surviving heirs scattered all over the globe.

Not all of the job's difficulties were bureaucratic in nature. The hardest part related to the heart, as we learn from Pomrenze's successor, Captain Isaac Bencowitz. Also a linguist and in civilian life a chemist, he served from April 1946 until October of that year. He recorded his feelings about the assignment in his diary.

> I would walk into the loose document room to take a look at the things there and find it impossible to tear myself away from the fascinating piles of letters, folders, and little personal bundles. Not that what you held in your hand was so engrossing, but rather what the next intriguing item might be. Or, in the sorting room, I would come to a box of books which the sorters had brought together, like scattered sheep into one fold—books from a library which once had been in some distant town in Poland, or an extinct *Yeshiva*. There was something sad and mournful about these volumes . . . as if they were whispering a tale of yearning and hope long since obliterated.
>
> I would pick up a badly worn Talmud with hundreds of names of many generations of students and scholars. Where were they now? Or rather, where were their ashes? In what incinerator were they destroyed? I would find myself straightening out these books and arranging them in the boxes with a personal sense of tenderness as if they had belonged to someone dear to me, someone recently deceased.
>
> There were thousands of loose family photographs without any identification. How dear all these tokens of love and gentle care must have been to someone and now they were so useless, destined to be burned, buried, or thrown away. All these things made my blood boil. . . . How difficult it is to look at the contents of the depot with the detachment of someone evaluating property or with the impersonal viewpoint of scholarly evaluation.[15]

DISTRIBUTION OF HEIRLESS CULTURAL PROPERTY

Baron's commission evolved into the Jewish Cultural Reconstruction Foundation, and was recognized by the United States
Military Government as the official agency to receive and dis-
tribute the heirless cultural property found in Germany. Under
Executive Director Dr. Hannah Arendt (1906–1975), it
functioned from mid-1949 until 1951.

The foundation's reports document the results of its efforts.[16]
Only established libraries and museums were to receive the
properties. The ratio of distribution was, roughly, 40 percent to
Israel, 40 percent to the Western Hemisphere, including the
United States, and 20 percent to other countries, including
Great Britain. In Israel, the principal beneficiary was the library
of Hebrew University, which had sent Shlomo Shunami, its
expert bibliographer, to assist in the sorting of the material prior
to shipment to Israel. He wrote a fascinating account of his
eight-month stay at the Offenbach depot.[17]

Before shipment to the various countries, the U.S. Army in
Germany loaned 25,000 Hebrew books to the displaced-persons
camps for use in their educational activities. The sensitivity and
aid extended by the U.S. Army to the Jewish displaced persons
was movingly acknowledged when, in 1948, the U.S. Army
helped publish a nineteen-volume offset edition of the Talmud,
the classic texts of Jewish law and tradition. In response, the
rabbinical chairman of the Central Committee of Liberated
Jews, the organizational arm of the displaced persons in the U.S.
Zone,[18] prefaced the edition with the following dedication:

This edition of the Talmud is dedicated to the United States Army.
The Army played a major role in the rescue of the Jewish people
from total annihilation, and after the defeat of Hitler bore the major
burden of sustaining the DPs of the Jewish faith. This special edition
of the Talmud published in the very land where, but a short time
ago, everything Jewish and of Jewish inspiration was anathema, will
remain a symbol of the indestructibility of the Torah. The Jewish
DPs will never forget the generous impulses and the unprecedented
humanitarianism of the American forces, to whom they owe so
much.

In the name of the Rabbinical Organization

Rabbi Samuel A. Snieg
Chairman and Chief Rabbi of the U.S. Zone[19]

Not all heirless Jewish material and property was properly routed through the Offenbach depot and Jewish Cultural Reconstruction Foundation. In some cases, use of unauthorized channels resulted in no real harm, as with the library of the prestigious *Klaus* synagogue of Mannheim. Its last rabbi was the learned Isaac Unna (1872–1948), whose Talmud classes were attended by Dr. Max Gruenewald, the scholarly community rabbi of Mannheim. In a recent interview, Rabbi Gruenewald told the story of how that library came to its current home in Cincinnati.[20] The *Klaus* library fortunately had been removed from the synagogue before the Nazis did it any damage, and spent the war years in storage at the municipal *Schlossbibliothek* ("Castle library"). After the war, the library was turned over to Rabbi Henry Tavel, a U.S. Army chaplain stationed in nearby Heidelberg. On his own authority, he shipped it to his alma mater, the Hebrew Union College in Cincinnati.

In other cases, individuals had come into possession of Jewish property illegally, and were trying to bypass regulations in order to realize a personal profit. Sometimes such crimes were thwarted. In May 1950, a Berlin bookdealer offered Alexander Marx a beautifully illustrated manuscript for the sum of $5,000. As is customary, Marx requested that the manuscript be mailed to him on approval. Former Seminary Librarian and Chancellor Gerson Cohen tells the rest of the story:

> As soon as the velvet-bound manuscript was in his hands, he sensed that it was not completely unfamiliar. Immediately, Dr. Marx, whose knowledge of Hebrew manuscripts was legendary, recognized certain pages as having been reproduced in an 1898 article, where they were identified a part of *Rothschild Manuscript 24*. Tempting as the item must have been to a librarian, Dr. Marx immediately notified the U.S. State Department, and the Rothschild family, of his discovery. Correspondence confirmed the fact that this was indeed a manuscript stolen from the Roth-

schild collection in Paris by the Nazis. The State Department thanked Dr. Marx for his help in restoring the prayer book to its rightful owner; the Rothschild family requested that he bring it back personally. They were understandably unwilling to trust the precious book to any common carrier. In the summer of 1951, Dr. Marx complied with their request and the story ended.

Fifteen years later, a new chapter was added. Baron Edmond de Rothschild, of the French branch of the famous family, presented the Seminary library with a fifteenth-century illuminated manuscript, in an almost perfect state of preservation. That manuscript has had a privileged position in our collections. First, it is extraordinarily beautiful. Second, it is rare, having been written in Florence in 1492 by the scribe Abraham Judah of Camerino. And finally, in presenting it Baron de Rothschild referred graciously to Dr. Marx's role in restoring the first manuscript to his family, and to the gratitude this act had inspired.[21]

THE ACHIEVEMENTS OF ALEXANDER MARX

When Alexander Marx came to the Seminary library in 1902, he found 5,000 printed books and three manuscripts in his care. In 1948, when he celebrated his seventieth birthday, he was in charge of the largest collection of Hebraica and Judaica in the world, with 140,000 books and 8,000 manuscripts.[22] In the year ending March 31, 1947, the library served 14,892 readers and visitors. In a year when the Seminary had need to borrow books from eleven institutions, seventy-nine libraries turned to the Seminary for interlibrary loans. Over the twenty years ending in 1947, the Seminary knew of 700 books and articles that were based in part on Seminary library materials.

The esteem which Marx had earned from colleagues everywhere was amply expressed at a special program on January 29, 1948, marking his seventieth birthday. All the Seminary-affiliated organizations participated, as did more than thirty other institutions, including Columbia, Harvard, Princeton, Yale, and universities from abroad. The occasion included the presentation by the Rabbinical Assembly of Marx's portrait, which still occupies a prominent place in the library. Professor Lieberman addressed the assembly and, in honor of the occasion, edited the Marx Jubilee volume, published in 1950.

But this recognition hardly marked the end of Marx's contributions. Yet to come was the pleasure of receiving still more priceless manuscripts. In 1923, the Seminary had purchased the remarkable Elkan Adler collection. After Adler's death in 1946, Alan M. Stroock, chairman of the board of directors, purchased 500 manuscripts and 300 single leaves and fragments from the Adler estate. He presented the new treasures to the library in memory of his father, Sol M. Stroock, who had also served as the Seminary's board chairman.

In thanking Stroock for the valuable donation, Marx noted that among the items received was a copy of the oldest commentary on the Mishnah. It was the same copy, Marx wrote, that had been offered to him many years earlier but that he was unable to buy because he did not have the funds. Only the Hebrew University of Jerusalem owned another copy.[23]

The Stroocks maintained a close connection to Marx through the historian Abraham Berliner (1833–1915), who had been one of Marx's teachers at the Hildesheimer Rabbinical Seminary in Berlin and was, by coincidence, a great-uncle of Sol Stroock. As a result, the library received some unusual material from the Stroocks. For example, Sol Stroock donated the letters of Berliner. The painter Hermann Struck (1876–1944) was also a member of the family. After his death in Israel, his widow sent some interesting family documents to the Seminary library.

Marx continued to cope with library problems as well, especially such recurring problems as shortages of space and funds. Competition for scarce funds made it impossible to install four additional cases in the manuscript room for the Adler collection. The library report of March 10, 1949, lists the needs then considered most urgent: the binding of new manuscripts; the acquisition of additional rare books; the periodic publication of recent acquisitions; photographic copies of important manuscripts in European libraries; and slides, photographs, and copies of the manuscript treasures of the Seminary library, so that a greater public could make use of the material. Another priority was the compilation of a library catalog by Hebrew authors. At the time, the Hebrew divisions of the library were arranged by title only, which was a serious handicap in view of the growth of modern Hebrew literature.

Another pressing matter for Marx's attention was finding a successor to Boaz Cohen, assistant librarian for over twenty-five years.Cohen's wish to devote all of his time to teaching and research coincided with Marx's desire to curtail his range of activities due to advancing age. The solution was a reorganization of responsibilities. Dr. Marx assumed the newly created position of director of libraries, and remained directly in charge of manuscripts and rare book collections. And Rabbi Gerson D. Cohen, a 1948 Seminary graduate, was named librarian as of September 1, 1950, when he was to take over general library operations.

THE FINKELSTEIN STYLE

The willingness to meet head-on the need for change, within and outside the Seminary, was a hallmark of the Finkelstein presidency. Under Finkelstein, the institution entered a period of vigorous expansion, the scope of which may be gauged by the number and range of the departments reporting to the board of overseers at their meeting on March 14, 1949. They were: Rabbinical Assembly; United Synagogue; Museum; Eternal Light; the University of Judaism, the Seminary's school on the West Coast; Adult Jewish Education; Library; and Inter-Group Activities.

At that meeting, chaired by former New York Governor Herbert H. Lehman (1876–1963), the chairman of the library committee, Louis M. Rabinowitz (1887–1957), urged increased fundraising efforts to meet the growing needs of the library. He himself had been a most generous supporter, donating many rare books and special materials to the library; he also sponsored the Institute in Rabbinics, which prepared scientifc editions of rabbinic works.

The growing visibility of the Seminary on the American scene was illustrated by Finkelstein's appearance on the cover of *Time* magazine on October 15, 1951. The feature detailed his leadership role in the Conservative movement. Further developments

at the time led to a reorganization of the top Seminary administration with Finkelstein assuming the new post of chancellor and
delegating administrative duties to two vice-chancellors and the
Seminary provost.

No longer tied down to day-to-day duties in New York,
Finkelstein embarked on a three-month-long trip to Israel in the
spring of 1952. As a result of this trip, arrangements were set
into motion for an Israel Center for Seminary students. A few
years later, in 1958, ground was broken for the American
Student Center, and from then on each rabbinical student was
required to study there for one year.

To all involved, and especially to Alexander Marx, the
highlight of the trip was a special convocation on May 25, 1952,
at which the honorary degree of Doctor of Hebrew Letters was
conferred upon David Ben-Gurion (1886–1973), the Prime Minister of Israel. Marx made the presentation, which was meant as
a personal tribute to Ben-Gurion and also as a symbolic expression of the Seminary's support of Israel.

Taking pride in this official function and deriving satisfaction
from transacting library business in Israel, Marx also experienced joy on this visit to Jerusalem as he became reacquainted
with his family, including his brother-in-law Shmuel Yosef
Agnon (1888–1970), the famous poet and Nobel Prize winner of
1966.

Upon his return to New York, Marx concentrated on his work
with manuscripts. He was particularly anxious to make progress
on his critical edition of the complete *Seder Olam*, part of which
had been his Ph.D. dissertation. In this undertaking, he was
ably assisted by one of his favorite students and now his close
associate, librarian Gerson Cohen. Sadly, Marx did not live to
see its publication. He died at the age of seventy-five on December 26, 1953. Gerson Cohen describes the last few weeks of
Marx's productive life in his response to a concerned correspondent:

> With reference to your inquiry concerning Doctor Marx, I can tell
> you that the passing of Professor Louis Ginzberg on November 11,

1953 was a great blow to him. His lifelong friend and colleague was the last of his close associates who had begun teaching with him in 1903. On December 17, 1953, the widow of Professor Israel Davidson, died, and after Professor Marx returned from the funeral he felt ill and went to bed. He was taken to the hospital on Wednesday December 23rd, and passed away on Shabbos morning, December 26, 1953. He died without suffering physical pain and in the thick of work, for he had many plans for the Library in which he was deeply involved to the very last. We indeed feel the loss keenly as you can well understand.[24]

Serving as a magnificent memorial to Marx was the Seminary library, consisting of 153,000 volumes and 8,500 manuscripts at the time of his death. After Marx's death, the personal libraries of three great friends and colleagues—Davidson, Ginzberg, and Marx—were combined, becoming a separate collection in their names. Thus were added to the library 4,000 volumes from Ginzberg, whose major strength lay in the area of Talmud, Codes, and Responsa; 13,000 volumes of the Marx library, bought for the Seminary by a number of friends, and covering the fields of Jewish history, literature, and bibliography; and the many books from the Davidson collection, especially strong in medieval Hebrew literature, which were on permanent loan to the Seminary from the College of the City of New York.

Chapter Five

Marx's Successors

When Marx retired from the position of librarian, the job changed radically. The once-in-a-lifetime opportunity to build a great library from scratch had been given to Marx. He had devoted fifty years to the task, and met the challenge magnificently. The challenges that remained were of a different order.

For Marx's immediate successors, the primary task was to bring the library's somewhat idiosyncratic procedures in line with modern library science. They needed to formulate new policies for purchasing, cataloging, book maintenance, and reader services.

GERSON D. COHEN

Gerson Cohen accepted the position of librarian reluctantly, and only at the strong urging of Chancellor Finkelstein. More interested in teaching and research than librarianship, he nonetheless took his library duties seriously. Early on, he visited other research libraries, including the mammoth Library of Congress in Washington, to learn about their internal operations. This perspective informed his first report to the board of overseers, presented in 1951 while Marx was director of libraries.

In this report, he was able to identify clearly problems particular to the Seminary library.[1] He noted that many books were in disrepair, and without new bindings could not be made available to readers. Over 8,000 books remained uncataloged, as did the thousands of books from the *Stuermer* collection, acquired under the Jewish Cultural Reconstruction program.[2] The chronic problem of space was worsening. As a result, several hundred manuscripts were being stored in cases outside the Rare Book Room.

Cohen also identified areas for growth. He was particularly interested in adding to the library's holdings in the literature of the new State of Israel. And following the initiative of Provost Moshe Davis, Cohen hoped to make the library a repository of source material in the field of American Jewish history. In particular, Cohen and Davis saw the Seminary Archives as the natural place for the records of Conservative congregations.[3] Unfortunately, lack of space and funds slowed the systematic collection of data pertaining to the Conservative movement.

In his first report after Marx's death, presented in 1954, Cohen proposed selling those volumes not needed by the Seminary or its West Coast branch, the University of Judaism.[4] A precedent existed in the sale of duplicates from the Enelow collection to Harvard University in the 1930's. The proceeds had been used for additional purchases. When Cohen made his suggestion some twenty years later, the sale of extra volumes would provide not only funds but also space. The sale was organized by a commercial outlet, the Ideal Bookstore, which had sold books for the library of Columbia University and some Columbia professors.

Cohen worked out a general policy governing library acquisitions. For the board's library committee, he reiterated the principles behind Marx's book buying. First and foremost, the library collection was to support Seminary faculty and students in their studies; secondly, the library was to be a world-class center for Jewish research.[5] To accomplish these complementary aims, library acquisitions were to strengthen the collection in the subjects taught in Seminary courses, that is, in Bible, Talmud, Rabbinics, Jewish law, liturgy, philosophy, history, and bibliography. Concentration in these areas was easily justifiable because many excellent general libraries in the city made their holdings on other subjects available through interlibrary loan.

Under Cohen, important donations continued to be made to

the library. For example, in 1955, the library acquired the Samaritan Bible, a 15th-century manuscript of 643 well-preserved pages, written in the Samaritan alphabet with a parallel translation in the Arabic. As early as 1931, Marx had been interested in buying it from the Deinard estate, but did not have the money. Now it was bought jointly by Harry K. Cohen of Philadelphia, and Dr. Harry G. Friedman, Louis M. Rabinowitz, and Julius Silver, all of New York City, and presented to the library in Marx's memory. Other significant gifts included the library of Rabbi Samuel Schulman of Temple Emanu-El. Admiral Lewis L. Strauss, president of the Seminary's Library Corporation, donated microfilms of Hebrew manuscripts in the collection of the Bibliotheca Escorial of Madrid, Spain. Additional microfilms were obtained through friends of the late Louis Ginzberg, in whose name a memorial collection had been established. To this collection as well were added rabbinic manuscripts from the Bodleian library, the Vatican library, and the Taylor-Schechter Genizah collection of the Cambridge University library.

NAHUM M. SARNA

Despite success as librarian, Cohen was anxious to return full time to teaching and research.[6] As a result, Dr. Finkelstein named Nahum M. Sarna chief librarian as of Steptember 1, 1957. Sarna was to serve as assistant professor of Bible at the Teachers Institute, lecturing ten hours a week, as well.

Born in England, he had received his B.A. and M.A. from the University of London and, in 1946, graduated from London's Jews' College with the Minister of Religion diploma. For several years, he was lecturer in Hebrew at London University, and he spent 1949 and 1950 in Israel. In the United States since 1951, he held a fellowship in Semitic languages and Biblical studies at Dropsie College, Philadelphia, where he earned his Ph.D. in 1955. He also served as an assistant professor of Bible at Gratz College, Philadelphia, for several years. Beginning in September 1956, he was visiting lecturer in Bible at the Seminary's Teachers Institute.

Sabato Morais,
Founding President

Solomon Schechter,
Second President

Cyrus Adler,
Third President

Jacob H. Schiff,
Philanthropist and
major supporter

Mayer Sulzberger,
Principal Architect
of Library

Louis Marshall,
Chairman of Seminary
Board of Directors

LIBRARY
OF THE
JEWISH THEOLOGICAL SEMINARY
OF AMERICA

PRESENTED BY
MORTIMER L. SCHIFF

Mortimer L. Schiff,
Organizer of
Library Corporation

Elkan N. Adler,
World traveller
and bookcollector

עקד הספרים של אלחנן
הכהן אדלר

Linda R. Miller,
Donor of
Enelow Collection

Solomon Goldman,
Rabbi, scholar,
communal leader

LIBRARY
OF THE
JEWISH THEOLOGICAL SEMINARY
OF AMERICA

ALEXANDER MARX MEMORIAL LIBRARY

Alexander Marx,
Seminary Librarian
1903-1954

Louis Finkelstein,
rth President 1940-1951
Chancellor 1951-1972

President Harry S. Truman, Viewing rare library book with
Chancellor Finkelstein and Professor Marx

The Fire of 1966

Student retrieving
damaged books

Volunteer drying water-logged
books by placing towels
between pages

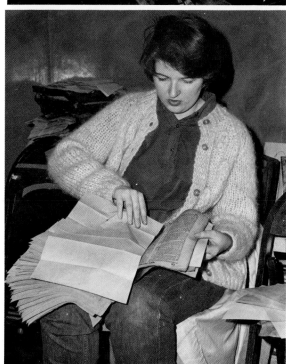

Drying water-logged books in seminary quadrangle

The Pre-Fab 1967-1983

Mayor John Lindsay, Inspecting fire damage together with Dr. Shama Friedman,
Acting Librarian, and Mrs. Edith Degani, Head of Technical Services

Pre-Fab's Cramped Interior

Groundbreaking of New Library, 1980, with Mayor Ed Koch, Chancellor G.D. Cohen, Boardmembers Alan M. Stroock, Simon H. Rifkind and Prog. Chairman Richard Ravitch

Nahum M. Sarna, Seminary Librarian 1957-1963

Gerson D. Cohen,
Seminary Librarian 1950-1957
Chancellor 1972-1986

Menahem Schmelzer,
Seminary Librarian
1963-1987

Ismar Schorsch,
Chancellor 1986

New Library

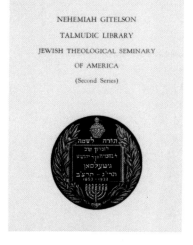

Bookplates of major collections

The cataloging and
restoration of the Seminary's
old Yiddish books
were made possible
through a generous grant
from
the Estate of Jacob Perlow.

Restored through the
generosity of the
Perlow Foundation

The restoration of this manuscript

was made possible

by the

Gustav Wurzweiler

Foundation

EDWARD CROWN
ARCHIVAL
FUND

This volume of Genizah fragments
was restored and preserved
through the generosity of the
Edward Crown Archival Fund

The
Aaron and Clara G. Rabinowitz
Fund

Bookplates of major foundations

Taking on the administration of the world's largest collection of Hebraica and Judaica did not faze Sarna. Before long, he grasped the special problems of the library, and then tackled them. Recalling his library years in a recent letter, he wrote:

> It soon became apparent to me that the world's greatest collection of Hebraica and Judaica, of manuscripts and rare books was in a parlous condition. Many thousands of books were uncataloged, and throughout the stacks, piles of unopened packages were to be seen. The physical conditions were primitive. There was no system of temperature and humidity control to protect the precious materials. The classification method was woefully antiquated. The library staff was competent, devoted, and hard-working, but was severely limited in its efficiency by the unsatisfactory conditions. Moreover, apart from the catalogers, the staff responsible for the day-to-day operation of the library, did not include anyone with a degree in library science. The worst feature was the scanty budget . . . salaries were far below the norm, and the library had no endowment. Purchases outside of the ordinary acquisitions had to be funded through special ad hoc fundraising from friendly, interested individuals.[7]

To improve this state of affairs, Sarna quickly made several critical staffing decisions. He appointed an administrative assistant with a Master of Library Science, Judith Ginsberg. She served extremely ably from 1958 to 1968. Sarna also praises Roberta Barkan, also a Columbia graduate with a degree in Semitics, who served for a few years as a researcher. In order to make maximum use of Anna Kleban's many talents, he created a new position, coordinator of field activities. In this capacity, Kleban, who had joined the library staff in 1925, provided the library with important public relations services. Sarna also added a second cataloger of Hebrew books, Rabbi Judah Brumer. In 1960, Rabbi Brumer became cataloger of manuscripts, a post he still fills and from which he has contributed an eight-volume catalog detailing more than 2,500 manuscripts, most of which are in Hebrew, but some are in Arabic, Ladino, and Persian.

But Sarna's work was just beginning. As he recalls:

It was not long before it became clear that no substantial progress could be made unless a thorough professional survey of the entire situation would be undertaken by an outsider. Accordingly, I persuaded the administration to enlist the services of a distinguished scholar in this specialized field. Maurice Tauber, Professor of Library Science at Columbia University, was engaged to undertake the task. He spent several months examining every aspect of our library, its resources, use, readers' services, its quarters and equipment, the technical service, the administration and personnel, and its financial situation. The results of his arduous efforts were embodied in a 153 page report that contained painstaking analysis, much critical observation and far-reaching recommendations in the greatest detail.[8]

In a library report of 1959, Tauber's recommendations appear.[9] He urged the erection of a new and modern library building, the recataloging of the manuscript collection, and the air-conditioning of the manuscript room and the reading room. The Tauber report was greeted with great interest, and many other libraries requested copies.[10]

The response of the Seminary to the report is remembered by Sarna in his letter:

> The immediate impact of this Tauber report was small because it demanded considerable sums of money to implement. In the course of time several important improvements were made. Funds were obtained to preserve the priceless collection of Genizah fragments. A bindery was established on the premises. I was fortunate to be able to recruit a refugee bookbinder who owned his own equipment.

Here Sarna refers to Hyman Erlich, a skilled craftsman who had owned a small bindery and sold its equipment to the Seminary. He worked with this equipment at the Seminary until his retirement in 1981. Sarna continues:

> Unfortunately, it was not possible to improve the accommodations for readers, staff, books and other materials. Professor Tauber frequently expressed his personal opinion that the ten-tier-tower used to house the collection was not only lamentably inadequate in itself but was also a fire trap. Alas, it took a disastrous conflagration to provide the impetus for new quarters worthy of the great treasures of the JTS library.

Under Sarna, the library's holdings increased by 30,000 printed books and 1,000 manuscripts, bringing the total to 200,000 printed volumes and 10,000 manuscripts. These substantial increases were due in large part to the energetic leadership of Julius Silver, chairman of the library committee during the Sarna years. Silver founded Friends of the Library, a group to help support library activities. One of the group's major accomplishments was acquiring the Judah A. Joffe Yiddish collection, consisting of more than 1,000 rare printed books and 25 manuscripts of early Yiddish literature. Joffe was persuaded to sell the collection to the Seminary by his friend Isaac Rivkind, the library's scholarly chief of Hebraica. A catalog of this collection is now being prepared by Rabbi Jerry S. Schwarzbard.

Sarna continued assembling on microfilm the Judaica collections of major libraries throughout the world, enabling scholars to examine the texts without having to travel to the originals. He also inaugurated a program of laminating, by a special Japanese method, the Cairo Genizah fragments.

The position of assistant librarian was still unfilled, and Sarna, like Cohen before him, bore a heavy load of work and responsibility. After six years at the head of the library, Sarna was ready to return to teaching and writing, and the search for a new librarian began anew.

The search began well. While visiting Professor Edward Y. Kutscher of Hebrew University, Seminary Provost Bernard Mandelbaum was told of Menahem Schmelzer, a young librarian at the Hebrew University. After a quick breakfast interview at the King David Hotel, Jerusalem, Mandelbaum immediately offered Schmelzer a research fellowship to assist in the library for the academic year 1961–62. At the urging of his wife, Ruth, Schmelzer agreed to come for the one year. Almost twenty-five years later, Dr. Schmelzer heads the library still.

MENAHEM SCHMELZER
In June 1962, Finkelstein announced Schmelzer's appointment as assistant librarian. The Hungarian-born scholar had been

educated at Budapest's Jewish Theological Seminary and University. He had studied as well at the University of Basel in Switzerland. In 1960, he received his Master of Arts degree from the University of Copenhagen, in Denmark, and a diploma from the Library School of Denmark. After working at the Royal Library of Copenhagen, he spent a year at the Hebrew University library in Jerusalem.

Foremost among Schmelzer's many strengths was his professional library training, coupled with his extensive experience in library work. With Dr. Sarna's resignation in 1963, Schmelzer became associate librarian and then head librarian. At the same time, he continued his studies in medieval Hebrew literature, earning a Doctor of Hebrew Literature degree in 1965 and a faculty appointment in this field.[11]

At the beginning of his tenure, Schmelzer spent considerable time reorganizing the Hebrew collection of the Rare Book Room. A special grant from the Wurzweiler Foundation impelled work on the restoration of manuscripts and rare books. The grant made possible the encasing of more than 3,000 Genizah fragments in airtight plastic envelopes and special binders, to protect them from disintegration.

The cataloging was speeded by the arrival of Rabbi Jacob Haberman, who, in 1961, obtained his Master of Library Science from Columbia University. In 1964, Dr. Alexander Tobias, a rabbinic scholar, arrived from England to assist in the cataloging of manuscripts.

And at long last, reason to hope for a solution to the vexing space shortage was at hand. In 1964, the board of overseers declared that the Seminary's number-one priority was a new library building. To reach this goal, the board announced a five-year campaign to raise $35 million. The new library building was planned for a site near the Teachers Institute where two Seminary-owned residential properties then standing would be razed. The proposed structure would house 400,000 volumes, double the size of the collection at the time. But the plan did not proceed smoothly. On April 18, 1966, a fire broke out in the Seminary tower, consuming 70,000 volumes and damaging more than 100,000 others with fire and water.

Chapter Six

The Fire of '66

by Barry D. Cytron

On the morning of October 26, 1966, a car left the Seminary grounds with Rabbi David Kogen at the wheel, and Louis Finkelstein and Menahem Schmelzer at his side. Filling the trunk of the car were boxes upon boxes, each measuring about three feet long and one foot deep. The car moved toward its destination, a Jewish cemetery up in the Hudson Valley. As he drove, Rabbi Kogen reflected on the circumstances that had impelled him and his passengers to set out on this particular journey.

It had all begun on Monday morning, April 18, 1966. The city had awakened to a beautiful spring day. The Morningside Heights area where the Seminary was located was alive with motion as thousands of students and faculty headed off for a new week of classes.

At 10:15 that morning, Professor Saul Lieberman, the Rector of the Seminary and one of its great luminaries, took a break

Rabbi Barry D. Cytron of Adath Jeshurun Congregation, Minneapolis, Minnesota, was a Seminary student at the time of the fire. He has also told the story of the fire in a book for young people entitled *Fire! The Library Is Burning!* (Lerner Books, 1988), from which this chapter is adapted.

Rabbi Cytron used the following sources in preparing this chapter: *Danzig, 1939, Treasures of a Destroyed Community, 1980,* published by the Jewish Museum in conjunction with the exhibit of the same name; Robert DeCandido, "Preserving Our Library Materials," *Library Scene,* September 1979; David Dempsey, "Operation Booklift," *Saturday Review,* April 15, 1967; *New York Times,* April 18, 1966; personal interviews with members of Seminary faculty and administration, in the spring of 1982; published and unpublished reports of the Seminary library and administration, including the 1984 Report of the Chancellor.

from his studies and peered out his office window. He thought he spotted a small dark cloud floating skyward from a tiny opening in the Seminary's Library tower. Sensing something seriously amiss, Professor Lieberman called the switchboard operator, who in turn relayed a call to the New York City Fire Department.

Thus begins a story of remarkable dimensions. For what the late Professor Lieberman had spotted was the first evidence of an enormous fire eating its way through the Seminary library. This raging fire would have destroyed completely the greatest collection of Jewish books ever assembled—had it not been for the courageous efforts of New York's firefighters, and the giving, working hands of thousands of New Yorkers who came to help that day, and in the months that followed.

The New York Fire Department responded to the Seminary operator's call within minutes. But the firemen were quickly stymied in their attempt to bring the fire under control. Only sixteen tiny windows, and one stairwell, opened into the ten-story tower where the library was situated. To make matters worse, the floors which housed the stacks were not solid, but had been built of open metal grating. This construction allowed the fire to move unhindered from floor to floor, so that the tower was functioning like a gigantic chimney.

As soon as Fire Chief Alfred Eckert recognized what he was facing, he made several decisions which seem, in retrospect, to have been brilliant. Convinced that acid discharges from chemical extinguishers would ruin any books his men might save, Eckert decided to use only water in combatting the flames. But how could he minimize the water damage, while at the same time arresting the rapidly spreading flames?

It was then that Eckert hit upon the idea of turning the library building's horrendous design feature—open metal flooring—to advantage. He dispatched oxygen-masked firefighters to the highest floor to which they could safely ascend. There they were to spread canvas tarpaulins across the top of hundreds of shelves of books. At the same time, hook and ladder trucks were positioned adjacent to the building. Under intense pressure, fire-quenching water was forced into the highest openings in the tower. Eckert's aim was to create a massive waterfall throughout the cavity of the tower, hoping that it would douse the flames spreading unchecked.

The plan worked, though not immediately, and not without sacrifice by the hundreds of firefighters. Nearly seventy of the men had to be treated for exhaustion and smoke inhalation as they battled the fire all that afternoon and into the evening. But with the help of additional men and equipment sent from other stations—thirty-five fire companies in all—Eckert was able to declare the fire officially "under control" by about seven o'clock that evening.

Some nine hours had elapsed. Not much time, but it was sufficient for a group of people to come forward who would see the Seminary through the months to follow. At the top of the list was David C. Kogen, the vice chancellor for administration. Under his calm, reasoned direction, an emergency committee came to life. The group consisted of Menahem Schmelzer, the highly regarded head librarian; Jessica Feingold and Carlotta Damanda, who worked together at the Institute for Religious and Social Studies, the Seminary's outreach department; and Marjorie Wyler, who was in charge of the Office of Public Information.

The committee met constantly throughout that first day. Initially, its concern was to ensure the safety of the staff, faculty, and students of the school. As the day, and then weeks, wore on, the committee took responsibility for the hundreds of decisions confronting the Seminary administration: assessing the damage to the library, planning for the rescue of the books which remained, recruiting the hands and financial resources which would be required, while all the while trying to maintain normalcy throughout the complex, which was the central address for the entire Conservative movement as well as home for thousands of students studying in rabbinic, cantorial, under-graduate, and even high school classes.

The committee knew it was essential for the many units of the Seminary campus to continue functioning as regularly as possible in the face of the emergency. But the first visit Schmelzer made to the blackened stacks convinced the committee that their first priority, other pressing tasks notwithstanding, was to mobilize every person available to assist in the library rescue.

What Schmelzer discovered as he walked through his library on Tuesday morning, accompanied by Fire Chief Eckert and his men, was a disaster beyond his worst nightmares. The top three floors of the tower were gone. No books. No pages. Just ashes. It was only as Schmelzer and his guides wound their way down the stairwell to the lower floors that they discovered that there was some semblance of the library still intact. To be sure, none of the books had escaped being hit by some of the thousands of gallons of water which had been poured in. Some were drenched. Others were merely moist to the touch. What Schmelzer realized at that moment was that a plan was needed to pull all the books which remained, inspect and dry them, and maybe, with luck, return the library to a usable state.

Within hours after receiving Schmelzer's report from that initial tour, the committee sent out the word for help in emptying the tower and salvaging the remains. By early Wednesday morning, there were thousands of hands—students and faculty, from the Seminary and the other Morningside institutions, along with others who had phoned to offer assistance. Librarians from the schools in the area graciously dispatched wagon carts and temporary shelving. Neptune Van Lines delivered truckloads of cartons to use in moving and storing the books.

With people and materials in place, "Operation Booklift," as it came to be known, began. It was a tedious process of pulling filthy, waterlogged volumes from the foul-smelling stacks, book by book, and passing them along into the fresh air and light. Emptying the stacks required nearly two weeks of constant effort by the volunteers, who found themselves physically exhausted by the labor and emotionally drained as they felt the extensive damage sustained by the books which passed through their hands.

Though the volunteers originally tried to keep the books in some sort of order as they came down the lines, the librarians eventually decided to forgo that effort. For while the librarians were keenly aware that maintaining an orderly arrangement was essential in making the library accessible, they knew that a much more serious threat confronted their library than merely the lack of order. It was the danger of mold.

Books are highly susceptible to mold. Publishers generally specify that the paper used in production be strengthened with the addition of a natural additive, "sizing." Contact with water sets off a chain reaction, causing bacteria to feast on the pages. If unchecked, mold can rot a book's pages in a short time. For that reason, as soon as the volumes were pulled from the stacks, provisions were made to dry them as best as possible.

Initially, that meant crudely setting the books up on end. Every spare room in the building, from Unterberg Auditorium to empty offices, was converted into a drying area. Tables were set up, so that horizontal space could be doubled. When the workers exhausted all available locations on the campus itself, they began moving the books up 122nd street, to a set of old apartment buildings adjacent to the Seminary. Years before, the Seminary had purchased those buildings in expectation of demolishing them and building a new library. But funds were needed elsewhere, and so the apartments, by 1966 mostly vacant, waited. Into these empty apartments the volunteers now began to pile books—on every flat surface they could find.

While this method worked in the first phase of Operation Booklift, it was neither the most efficient nor the most acceptable way to dry the volumes. Often it required shifting books around, in order to locate the wetter sections of the volume. Then, too, because the books were sitting in an unnatural position, the pages wrinkled badly, so that they might well turn out to be dry—but unreadable.

It was then that David Kogen came up with a second strategy to speed the drying along. He recalled that when he was a young child in Europe, his community's custom in preparing for Passover was to remove all the books from the houses and "air" them out, hoping that any leaven which might have fallen between the pages during the year would be whisked away by the breezes.

Under his direction, therefore, the Seminary Quadrangle was instantaneously transformed into a gigantic book-drying area. Rolls of paper were spread across the lawn. Students opened books and kept changing their positions as they dried. While the method proved effective, it required much open space and constant sunny weather—two conditions not always available in the middle of Manhattan. It was also very time consuming, drying relatively few books while some 170,000 volumes awaited attention. This last problem—the slowness of the method— concerned the committee most, for the committee was increasingly aware that time was one thing they were running out of in their fight against the mold.

It was then that the Seminary received what was the first of many generous offers to come from unlikely sources. In this instance, it came from the General Foods Corporation, the giant food company, located in Westchester County. That year the firm had developed a new product: freeze-dried coffee. The manufacturing process entailed brewing coffee and then using vacuum ovens to extract the water, leaving crystals which could be reconstituted into coffee with the addition of water. When executives at General Foods became aware of the library's plight, they contacted the Seminary, with the idea of providing some small test ovens, and technicians, to assist in determining whether the vacuum process could be applied to the books.

Many of the Seminary people hoped that freeze-drying would hold the key to saving the massive number of books still untouched. Though the process was useful, it turned out to be like every method used to date—much too time consuming. The ovens provided by General Foods were highly sophisticated, and extremely exacting in their requirements. Each book had to be measured for water content and size before the ovens could be powered up. The technicians and librarians did succeed together in saving a number of books; nonetheless, it was clear that what was still needed was some way of drying not just a select group of books but massive numbers.

No one is quite certain of the steps by which that method was finally hit upon. As best as some can recall, it was a visitor to the

Seminary, Bayla Bonder, who discovered it. Even if Bayla herself did not invent the method, she and many of her friends performed the tedious work which this method demanded. But tedious or not, it worked phenomenally well. The method involved taking paper towels and inserting one sheet between *every* two pages of a book—and then repeating the process two or three times until the book was completely dry.

Simple, and effective. Only two things were needed to make it work—hands and towels. Publicity attracted the helpers; savvy, the required paper towel suppliers. There were times, to be sure, when it seemed as if the Seminary were the only locale in all of New York with paper towels. And there was some truth to that. Manufacturers and wholesalers throughout the city diverted all the towels they could to 122nd Street and Broadway.

There were also hands aplenty. Perhaps this fact—the presence of so many diverse, caring people who helped—was the most extraordinary part of the entire library story. Volunteers from all over the area, Jews and Christians, young and old, came to help "interleaf," as the process soon came to be called. The library reading room, from where most of the work was being supervised, often resembled a huge picnic area, as strangers and friends sat across from one another and helped dry, page by page by page, most of the 170,000 books which had been pulled from the stacks.

As best it could, with words and gestures, the Seminary tried to express its gratitude to all who helped. Yet it often seemed to those who lent a hand that they should be the ones to say "thank you." For they were participating in a unique experience, saving not only a library but the record of a culture. The Seminary library was not just books, not just precious volumes collected from the past. No library is only that. Libraries are, rather, repositories of a people, the record of why they fall in love and why they fight, what they believe in and work for and hope towards. The Seminary library was just such a place—an unparalleled source of knowledge about the Jewish people, ever changing and growing. Those who came to help were thus not only saving books—they were working to rescue a civilization.

Not all of that civilization was saved, however. There were irretrievable losses sustained in the fire—though, fortunately, the most valuable books of the entire collection were kept in a totally isolated area of the Seminary campus, and as such were never in any danger from the fire. Still, many important collections were lost. These included:

> The papers and books of many Seminary scholars, including the personal collections of Cyrus Adler, Israel Davidson, Louis Ginzberg, and Alexander Marx.

> The Moritz Steinschneider collection, an irreplaceable library from the hands of the great Jewish bibliographer.

> The Zemachson and Zilberts collection of liturgical manuscripts.

> The Benaim collection of printed books and manuscripts from North Africa—a precious collection which was just being incorporated into the regular collection at the time of the fire.

> The personal papers of many famous Jewish personalities of the nineteenth and twentieth centuries, including Jacob Schiff, Alexander Kohut, Israel Goldstein, and Menachem Ribalow.

While these losses cannot be calculated, the unceasing efforts of Seminary personnel and volunteers served to limit the scope of what could have been a much greater disaster for both scholarship and history. But it was not only those people who joined to restore the library. So did many others, including a special group of children from the Riverside Church School, located just around the corner from the Seminary.

The preschoolers of the church school, it appears, had learned about the Seminary fire on the Monday of the fire. Under their teachers' guidance, the children decided to help by raising money to purchase new books. To do so, they spent the better part of a week baking cookies in the church kitchen, decorating and hand-wrapping each of them. Then they set up shop in the neighborhood, under a large sign which read "Help Save the Books." Their efforts were a huge success, netting the children $62.65.

Soon after, the children sent the following note to Chancellor Finkelstein:

Dear Doctor Finkelstein:

We are kindergarten children of Riverside Church in Room 615. We wanted to earn some money to help you replace your books. We thought of selling cookies. We baked cookies for four days. We baked about 500 cookies. We sold them for five cents each. We enjoyed doing it. We are sorry the books got burned.

Love . . .

The note was signed with the printed signatures of all twenty-five children from the church class, children with such names as Ichito, Ian, Marie Christine, and Kelly.

The correspondence files of the library contain the letter which the chancellor wrote in response. He thanked the children for their hard work, and noted how their generous act of helping was one of many such gracious gifts performed by persons and institutions throughout the country. "At a time of deep sadness," Finkelstein wrote, "this knowledge that so many people shared our loss and wanted to help has brought us great comfort."

The "deep sadness" which Louis Finkelstein wrote about to the children was nowhere more evident than on the October day when Kogen and his colleagues set forth on that ride to the cemetery. For they were headed there to complete one last ritual, as it were, associated with the fire—the burying of sacred texts.

Jewish law mandates that when sacred scrolls and other religious texts containing holy words can no longer be utilized for study and prayer they are to be buried. It was once customary for a synagogue or school to maintain a Genizah—a "hiding" or "treasure" room—to which such papers could be consigned. Today, more often, such texts are buried in a special section of a cemetery, often in an unmarked grave. It was to one such burial spot that Kogen was driving that morning.

But the boxes which were in the trunk of Kogen's car not only

contained scraps of sacred books with holy writing. Those boxes
also contained the remains of forty Torah scrolls, the remaining
scrolls of the destroyed Jewish community of Danzig. In 1938,
the Free City of Danzig, which at that time was home to some
10,000 Jews, was taken over by local Nazis. Attacks were
organized against the synagogues and other institutions, and the
leaders of the Jewish community soon realized that their time
was limited.

Accordingly, they undertook an active campaign to find ref-
uge for the entire Jewish population, away from the evil which
the Nazis were preparing for Europe's Jews. The leaders were
largely successful in completing arrangements, though approximately 1,200 older people were eventually seized and deported
by the Germans. Once the people were as secure as possible, the
leaders turned to the many institutional artifacts, ritual items,
and communal records gathered by the Danzig Jews over centuries of activity. In order to secure the safety of such physical
remains, the officials turned to Louis Finkelstein at the Seminary, who arranged for these sacred treasures to be stored in
New York.

Most of the communal property was safely protected at the
Seminary's Jewish Museum on Fifth Avenue. Ultimately, the
curators of the museum were to organize a poignant memorial to
the Jews of that Baltic seaport, an exhibition they entitled
Danzig: Treasures of a Destroyed Community. But the exhibit did not
contain any of the Torah scrolls shipped from the Danzig
synagogues, for they had been burned beyond recognition during the fire, stored as they had been on the library's tenth floor
for safekeeping.

The trip which Kogen, Finkelstein, and Schmelzer made that
autumn day to the cemetery was one marked by penetrating
sadness. Kogen can still recall the abject sense of loss felt by
himself and his passengers as they drove out and back. Yet the
trip also was an important symbol, a closure of sorts to the
events of those six months in the life of the Jewish Theological
Seminary.

The losses had run deep. The best estimates were that at least

15,000 books would never be replaced, and that the loss of personal notes and annotations contained in many of the destroyed volumes counted as far more of a loss than a destroyed book. But the disaster which struck the library had shown the unusual capacity of people to care. Children and adults, people of different religions and ethnic heritages, Jewish and Christian institutions, secular and religious foundations—all gave of themselves. The Ford Foundation made a substantial gift—its first ever to a religious academy. The Brooklyn Jewish Center donated its precious 5,000 volume library to help the Seminary replenish its collection. One gift after another flowed into the Seminary during those months after the fire.

In retrospect, the fire which swept through the library tower, followed by the extraordinary generosity of so many, came to represent living testimony to the Seminary emblem. Years before, in quest of an appropriate symbol for the school, the Seminary's leaders had chosen the Biblical words from the story of Moses in the wilderness: "And the Bush was not consumed." In 1966, amidst the great tragedy of the library fire, that symbol was brought to life. For all those volunteers who gave up thousands of hours during that lovely New York spring to rescue the books sent a profound message to the Seminary—the message that, though its famous library had once burned to flames, it, like the Burning Bush, would not be consumed.

Chapter Seven

Building Anew

by Edith Degani

By the fall of 1966 the rush was over and the volunteers had done as much as they could. Now it was the staff's turn to pick up the pieces and get the library functioning again. Classes were beginning, and it was imperative that the students be able to get the books they needed for their course work. This presented major difficulties. The fire had left the library with only a small area of shelving. The books that had survived the disaster were in total disarray. The first step toward the return to normalcy was to search for those books most needed by the students, and that would fit in the limited space available. When these were found and put in place, the semester could begin with at least minimal service available.

THE "PREFAB"
Thousands of books were stored all over the Seminary. They were in classrooms, in the gymnasium, even in a neighboring apartment house. Finding shelf space for these books became a high priority. The tower which had held the book stacks was now totally unusable and beyond repair. The staff, greatly augmented after the fire, needed space in which to work and get

Edith Degani has been a professional librarian since her graduation from Pratt Institute in 1943. After service with major New York libraries she joined the Seminary after the Fire of 1966, advancing to the post of assistant librarian.

started on the long process of restoration. A partial solution was reached with the erection of a prefabricated building, Quonset-hut style, in the courtyard of the Seminary. There was room in the prefab, as it came to be known, for some 120,000 volumes. The balance, about 30,000 at first, remained homeless until space was rented at a facility some distance from the Seminary. These "orphans" increased in quantity as the library's holdings grew from gifts and purchases. This overflow was moved several times until a semipermanent location was found in a nearby warehouse.

Meanwhile, the work of restoration continued in the prefab. All the books that had survived the fire had suffered damage from the flames, from smoke, or from water. Each book had to be examined separately to determine how it should be treated. Some books could be repaired in-house, while others required more extensive work by professional binders. Sometimes, by searching through the library's holdings, a copy in better condition could be found to replace the damaged book. Thousands of books went through this process of scrutiny and evaluation.

Many books had fallen apart and had survived only as fragments. Rabbi Joseph Weiss, a bibliographic specialist, concentrated on identifying over three thousand of these fragments. When he could find a library that owned the whole book, he contacted it and requested photocopies of the pages missing from the Seminary's copy. When the photocopy and the fragment were bound together, one more book had been restored and could be returned to the collection.

New cataloging procedures were introduced to make the books more accessible to the readers, but it was not an easy time for library users. Denied access to the shelves, they had to locate the books they wanted from the card catalog. They then had long waits until the books they wanted could be brought to them from the prefab. They were out of luck if the material they needed was stored off-campus in the warehouse. Despite the best efforts of everyone, staff as well as readers, the library was not functioning as well as it should.

MADE TO ORDER: A MODERN LIBRARY

For a long time, the Seminary leaders had been speaking of constructing a new library that would complete the Seminary's physical plant. Dr. Nahum Sarna, then Seminary librarian, wrote in an article on the library: "It is hoped that the greatest Jewish library of all time and one of the great cultural assets of the United States will, in the not too distant future, be housed in a building worthy of its importance and fully equipped to fulfill its role as the mecca of Jewish scholars."[1] When Dr. Gerson D. Cohen, also a former Seminary librarian, took office as chancellor in 1972, a new building was one of his prime objectives. Now that the need had become critical, serious attention was paid to bringing this about. Three distinguished architectural firms were invited to submit designs for a new building. A committee composed of representatives of all parts of the Seminary community studied the designs and selected the one deemed to be best suited. This was the proposal of the Gruzen Partnership, and approval was unanimous. The design called for a building of 75,000 square feet, of which 55,000 were assigned to the library. The rest of the space was reserved for a reception area, a 500-seat auditorium, and meeting rooms.

The first step to be taken was the demolition of two empty apartment houses that stood on the building site, and the leveling of the land. In November 1980, ground-breaking ceremonies were held in a large tent and attended by government officials, representatives of other institutions, and friends of the Seminary, many of whom had helped at the time of the fire. Mr. Charles Moerdler was among the speakers. As commissioner of buildings in the administration of Mayor John Lindsay, he had been the official who had given permission for the prefab to be built. Now he was aiding in its eventual demise. Construction began with excavating the site. Frequent dynamite blasts shook the neighboring structures. Noise and dust were everywhere, but there were few complaints, especially from the library staff, as the building gradually took shape.

In November 1981, dignitaries and guests met on the second floor of the new library for the ceremonial laying of the cornerstone. The walls were incomplete, scaffolding was all around, but it was the first time the new building had been used. To be there was a thrill for all who had been so deeply involved in its design and planning.

Progress continued, and as the building neared completion yet another ceremony was held. This took place in April 1982 while an unseasonable snowstorm raged outside. Each member of the Seminary's board of overseers carried a book from the old shelves and placed it on a shelf in the new building. There was no heat in the building that afternoon, but the excitement and the feeling of accomplishment generated their own warmth.

Finally, this building which had been a dream for so long was completed and could be occupied. The move into the new quarters began in January 1983. Done in stages, it was completed by the end of June of that year. By the use of detailed strategies, the entire move was accomplished with barely an interruption of service to the library's readers. The library was closed for three days only, and those were during school vacation.

After the books and staff had been moved from the prefab, the structure was razed. It had served well for sixteen years and had earned the distinction of being the longest-standing "temporary" building in the city of New York.

A major goal of the architects had been to achieve a blend between old and new, using modern architectural principles. They had even built a prototype of a brick wall sometime earlier to check on whether the new bricks would blend with the old ones as they aged. The building enclosed the campus on the east side, creating an attractive grass-covered courtyard in the middle of the campus. It was designed to give a stepped effect with a series of recessed floors, creating terraces on each level. Each setback was emphasized with skylights. The extensive use of glass provided a great deal of natural light throughout. Visitors entered in a large lobby, set off by an attractive terrazzo floor. A sweeping staircase led to the second floor, the main public floor of the library.

As the library opened its doors on July 5, 1983, a new era

began. Everything was in place. Books were on open shelves, available for browsing and selecting. Room was provided for half a million books on sturdy, shining shelves. Readers could choose from three types of seating: they could use one of the four reading rooms on the second and third floors; if they wanted more privacy, they could use an individual study carrel; for more relaxed reading, there were lounge chairs and tables. One lounge provided newspapers from around the world and periodicals in many languages. Students had asked that an area be provided in which they could study in groups, talking aloud as needed. Such a room was made available on the third floor, well equipped with reading stands to make easier the use of heavy Talmudic volumes. Excellent ambient lighting was provided throughout. Lights over the third-floor stacks were controlled by timers, a major energy-conservation measure. A room on the second floor offered state-of-the-art microform equipment. Amenities lacking in the old facility, such as washrooms and drinking fountains, were available on each floor. The July heat was controlled by a central air-conditioning system, a sharp contrast to the old days when readers sweltered in the summer weather.

The new building, however, did not yet contain the entire library. The rare book and manuscript collections, the great treasures that had given the library its outstanding reputation, were still to be moved. Before a single item could be relocated, complicated systems to safeguard the treasures had to be in place. While the rest of the library was protected against fire by sprinklers, a Halon fire-suppressant system was acquired for the area on the top floor of the building that would house the rare items. Such a system puts out a fire in seconds without damaging any material and without endangering anyone in the area. The installation requires the approval of the New York City Fire Department before the premises can be occupied. A sophisticated security system was installed to protect the collection. Special temperature and humidity controls, set at levels deemed best for the preservation of the ancient materials, were provided. In the old facility, visiting scholars and people from all over the world who came to use this collection were jammed into a small, uncomfortable room. Now, a luxuriously furnished reading room was provided. While the rest of the library was furnished in modern, white oak, this area was provided with traditional mahogany tables and Chippendale-type chairs, more in keeping with the nature of the material used there. When everything was in place, the rare books, the manuscripts, the graphic collection, and the archives were moved and installed in their new home. For the first time in many years, the entire library was under one roof.

During Hanukkah, on December 4, 1983, the building was dedicated in formal ceremonies held in the new Feinberg Auditorium. At these ceremonies, Chancellor Gerson D. Cohen said:

> This Library bespeaks an affirmation that the Jewish people, in the Diaspora, as well as in Israel, will continue to create and enrich our heritage by resting on a firm academic foundation and on fresh understanding of our past. May this Hanukkah of our library be the first day of a daily rediscovery and reaffirmation of the authentic spirit of Torah. May the Hanukkah of our library infuse our books and manuscripts with renewed life, even as the historic festival gave meaning to the work of liberation and purification of the Temple.

GROWING WITH COMPUTERS

Libraries, while remaining as repositories of ancient knowledge, continue to increase in size as new information appears. And, as new technological advances are made, libraries change their techniques for handling material. The development of microfilm and microfiche created new opportunities for the acquisition and storage of knowledge. So too has the advent of computers had a great impact on library systems. The Seminary library became part of the computer age in February 1978 when it joined a computerized library system known as the Online Computer Library Center (OCLC). Used mainly for cataloging, this tool has given the Seminary access to thousands of records entered by libraries throughout the United States. In turn it has permitted those libraries to learn of the Seminary's holdings. It has greatly speeded up the production of catalog cards and increased the efficiency of the entire operation. An IBM PC became the next step in computerization. Having Hebrew capability, it has proven to be an invaluable tool in word processing, with other uses for it being continually found.

Even greater computer technology is on the horizon. The Research Libraries Information Network (RLIN), another computerized cataloging system, has been developing Hebrew capability. When this innovation is operative, the Library will be able to enter all records, those in Hebrew as well as those in the Roman alphabet, in a national data base. At present, only Roman items may be entered.

The library, however, has still loftier aspirations. The long-range plan is to discard the current card catalog and replace it with an online computerized catalog. Tied to this computer would be all library procedures. Readers would no longer have to search in a card catalog to find the books they want. They would use one of the many terminals stationed in different parts of the library, and, using simple operations, find out if the library owns a specific book, where it is located, and whether or not it is charged out to someone else. The terminals would provide multiple access points, giving readers many more ways of locating the materials they want than are possible in a card catalog. This is still a dream, but, hopefully, a dream that will someday become a reality. While the initial cost would be substantial, the long-range benefits would be even greater. Computerization would promote access to the collections, facilitate collaboration with other research centers, and strengthen the Seminary's scholarly, educational, and cultural outreach. The Seminary library, often called the greatest Jewish library in the world for its magnificent collections, its manuscripts, its incunabula, could, in its second century, assume leadership in the new field of automated library service.

The library recovered from a nearly fatal disaster in 1966 to become a well-housed and well-run operation in 1986. It is better equipped than ever to fulfill its primary function of service to the students and faculty of the Seminary and to the Jewish community at large. Its doors are open to all who wish to enter. Its books and periodicals may be read by anyone who so desires. Its well-trained staff answers questions posed by all callers, regardless of who they may be. Verily the Seminary library thrives and is well. May it continue to be an inspiration to all.

Appendix A

AN UNPERFORMED CONTRACT: THE SALE OF BARON GUNZBURG'S LIBRARY TO THE JEWISH THEOLOGICAL SEMINARY OF AMERICA

by Michael Stanislawski

Almost immediately after Baron David Gunzburg, the scion of the *grande famille* of Russian Jewry, died on 10/23 December 1910, the fate of his famous library became an object of intense international interest, rumor, and intrigue. For in the baron's home in St. Petersburg was housed one of the greatest private libraries in the Russian Empire, if not in Europe as a whole, purchased by three generations of Barons Gunzburg through well-placed, and well-paid, agents around the globe. The assembled treasures were first housed in the Gunzburg residence in Paris, but were moved to St. Petersburg in the late 1880's to serve the research needs of Baron David, a noted specialist in all aspects of "Oriental" scholarship. Under his tutelage, the Hebraica and Semitica in the collection expanded to include approximately 2000 manuscripts and 5000 printed volumes, developing into possibly the most substantial Judaic library of its day, rivaling or surpassing that of the Bodleian Library at Oxford. Before his untimely death at the age of fifty-three, the baron delighted in displaying his enormously valuable rarities to visitors to his home and frequently used the manuscripts and rare books as texts in his seminars at the unofficial Jewish university which he founded in the Russian capital. In his will, Baron Gunzburg stipulated that his heirs must not allow the collection either to be broken up or to remain inaccessible to Judaic scholars; if it was not to be

---

Michael Stanislawski teaches history at Columbia University.

used by his family, it ought to be sold to an appropriate institution devoted to *Wissenschaft des Judentums*.[1]

It is not surprising, therefore, that only weeks after David Gunzburg's demise, speculation and concern over the disposition of his library spread through Russian Jewry and its offshoots in the United States and Palestine. As reports appeared in newspapers around the Jewish world that the Gunzburg collection might be destined for Oxford, Frankfurt, or New York, various Zionist spokesmen, for example, began to argue that the only appropriate place for the greatest Judaica library in the world was Jerusalem, and they began to organize a drive to effect that goal. That attempt, as well as the purchase of the Gunzburg library in 1917 by Russian Zionists for the nascent Hebrew University of Jerusalem, has been chronicled by a noted Israeli bibliographer.[2] Well-known, too, is the sad denouement of that tale: the refusal of the Soviet government to allow the library to leave for Palestine; the transfer of the collection to the Rumiantsev Museum in Moscow (later incorporated into the Lenin State Library); and the complex—and often most curious—history of the collection in the last several decades.[3]

One fascinating episode in this drama has, however, never been examined: the sale, in July 1914, of the Gunzburg library to the Jewish Theological Seminary of America. In his paean to the Barons Gunzburg published in his *Historishe Verk* in 1937, the Russian-Jewish historian Shaul Ginsburg noted in passing that such a sale had taken place, and that a contract signed by David Gunzburg's widow and the Seminary exists in the latter's archive.[4] In fact, the Seminary's archives contain not only such a contract, but a bulging file on the sale that includes another 183 documents detailing its origins, the complicated negotiations that culminated in the contract, and the tortuous—and legally hazy—conclusion of the affair.[5]

These hitherto unpublished materials not only establish conclusively that such a sale took place, but they contain valuable information on subjects as diverse as the history of the Gunzburg clan and the personalities and modus operandi of American Jewish leaders such as Jacob Schiff and Louis Marshall. But perhaps most interesting is the substantial light these materials shed on the self-conscious attempt of American Jewish leaders, already before World War I, to cast themselves as the natural heirs of the spiritual traditions of Russian Jewry. From this vantage point, the story of the competition over the Gunzburg library is a dramatic refraction of the intense, and little-studied, rivalry between the two daughter communities of Russian Jewry over the heritage of their parents.

Barely a fortnight after the death of Baron David Gunzburg, Zalman

Amitan, a Russian-Jewish merchant who had visited New York the previous summer and had been impressed with the library of the Jewish Theological Seminary of America, informed the Seminary that the Gunzburg family was interested in selling the Baron's library. Excited by this information, David Gunzburg's colleague in Judeo-Arabic studies at the Seminary, Professor Israel Friedlaender, wrote a long letter to Jacob Schiff, bringing to the philanthropist's attention this news, which was a matter of "vast importance for the Seminary, and I believe I may add for the intellectual development of American Jewry."[6] Playing on Schiff's well-established animosity towards the Tsarist regime, Friedlaender warned that efforts were already being made to secure the collection for the Russian government.

> Should these efforts succeed, incalculable and irreparable harm would result for the cause of Jewish learning and the honor of the Jewish people. For the greatest collection of Jewish treasures would then be concentrated in the hands of our enemies, and would be entirely lost to Jewish learning, as Russia, and particularly the capital, are practically inaccessible to Jewish scholars.[7]

On the other hand, if the Gunzburg collection, and particularly its invaluable manuscripts, could be acquired by the Seminary, the result would be a marvelous coup, catapulting its library to premier status within the Jewish scholarly world. But, Friedlaender hastened to add, more important than the benefits accruing to the Seminary from such a purchase would be the far-reaching consequences of such a sale for the whole of American Jewry.

> It is generally admitted that America is rapidly becoming the centre of the Jewish Diaspora and it is only befitting that it should also possess the largest collection of the spiritual treasures of our people. Such a collection, placed as it would be in the midst of the largest Jewish community in the world, would undoubtedly act as a powerful stimulus for Jewish knowledge and culture and could not but exert an ennobling influence on the development of American Judaism. It would help American Jewry to attain to that preeminence in the sphere of culture which it has already attained in so many other branches . . .[W]e are presented here with an opportunity, the like of which, it may be said without exaggeration, may not again occur for centuries.[8]

Schiff responded to this letter with an expression of interest coupled with the expectation that the cost of the library might be forbidding. But he did not rule out the possibility of carrying out confidential inquiries about the price being asked for the collection.[9]

Meanwhile, back in St. Petersburg, Amitan had already apprised Samuel Wiener, the Hebrew bibliographer at the Asiatic Museum of the Russian Academy of Sciences and a library aide to the late Baron, of the possible transfer of the Gunzburg materials to New York. Wiener quickly dispatched a letter to Alexander Marx, librarian and professor of Jewish history at JTS, urging that the Seminary was by far the most suitable locale for the library, and claiming that he had already convinced the Baroness to sell the collection to the Seminary for 600,000 rubles. He hoped that as a result of his critical role in this deal he would not only receive a fair commission, as was customary in such transactions, but also be employed in the library after its installation in New York.[10] Not to be outdone, Amitan nervously dispatched a letter and several postcards to Marx, broadly hinting that as the original broker of the offer he, too, should be rewarded for his efforts, as should the Gunzburgs' *major domo*.[11]

Marx, born and bred in Germany and trained in the Prussian artillery as well as the Berlin Rabbiner Seminar, was rather bewildered by what he termed these "Oriental" requests for "consideration," and turned for help to Judge Mayer Sulzberger, the noted American jurist and Hebraist, who had earlier donated the core of the Seminary's library. Sulzberger advised Marx to ignore these "sordid obstacles" and to deal directly with the Baroness after consulting with Seminary board members such as Schiff and Felix Warburg.[12] This Marx proceeded to do, but found that Jacob Schiff, for one, was very skeptical about the possibility of raising enough money to satisfy even half of what the Baroness reportedly sought. Schiff advised the disappointed Marx that the whole matter ought probably to be dropped.[13]

Marx was persistent however, and over the next year and a half slowly but methodically continued to build his case. Through Schiff's son-in-law, Felix Warburg, he was introduced to Baron Alexander Gunzburg (David's brother, who was related by marriage to the Warburgs), and with the Baroness's help he received a catalog of the library's Hebrew holdings.[14] By the end of 1912, Marx had enlisted in his cause Louis Marshall, the respected lawyer who was both the president of the American Jewish Committee and the chairman of the board of directors of JTS. Subtly rephrasing Friedlaender's earlier words to appeal to Marshall's own predilections, Marx wrote Marshall that

> What is most important is that American Jewry would (by the acquisition of the Gunzburg library) earn the gratitude of the whole nation, which would look with justifiable pride upon its supremacy also in the realm of literature and learning in this department. Our nation can never hope, with all the wealth at its disposal, to compete with Europe in other departments, say Greek or Latin . . . Hebrew alone is thus almost the only field in which we could still excel and win distinction.[15]

With Marshall's backing, Marx addressed a respectful letter to Baroness Mathilde Gunzburg, impressing upon her the fact that, as she must be aware, Jewish institutions of learning were not blessed with too much money, but "there is now a ray of hope that these difficulties may be overcome if the sum needed to secure the Gunzburg Collection would prove to be reasonable—say $100,000" (a third of the 600,000 rubles previously mentioned).[16]

In April 1913, the Baroness responded that her family would never allow her to part with the library for such a sum: "They will perhaps go down to 400,000 Rubles or 200,000 Dollars, but in no case less. It would disvalue the library." If her sons would interest themselves in Jewish manuscripts, never would she think of selling the collection, but her late husband's wish was that the books should be used and not hidden from those who could study them. "Certainly," she concluded, "it would be the right place for the library to be in Jewish Theological Seminary of America and under your inspection," but if it could only command so low a price, "I would rather keep it in memory of my late husband than disvalue this library that he loved so much."[17]

Distressed by this response, Marx answered the Baroness that there were no hopes at present that so large a sum could be raised from the Seminary's friends, but that he would be in touch if the situation changed for the better.[18] Behind the scenes he continued to lobby for the purchase of the Gunzburg rarities, and by the end of the year had evinced from Schiff a pledge to contribute a substantial sum—perhaps even $100,000—toward this end.[19] In March 1914, Marx received a new offer from the Baroness: she had explained to her family that they were asking too much, and they were prepared to come down to $125,000, but no less.[20] An ecstatic Marx then played his trump card, having Solomon Schechter, the renowned president of the Seminary, add his weighty touch to the effort. On 20 March 1914, Schechter wrote first to Louis Marshall that "generations to come will bless us for this great acquisition containing what is best in Israel's thought, and having secured it for the new world which is destined to become a Jewish world, just as well."[21] Then, to Jacob Schiff, Schechter invoked his loftiest rhetoric.

> It will be the consummation of the hopes and dreams of so many years of the best minds of American Israel. I see in it almost the finger of Providence when I think that this Library is the outcome of three generations of collectors, residing alternately in Russia, Germany, and France, and having their agents also directly or indirectly in the Orient and North Africa. But apparently its destination is to find its last haven in America, which also proves the asylum for refugees and sufferers from all these countries. When our ancient sages assured us in their hyperbolic language that wherever

Israel immigrated, the Schechina, or the Divine Presence came with them, I can only think that they had in mind such an event as will be brought about by the acquisition of this great Library, which embodies what is noblest and greatest in Israel's aspirations after the divine interpretation of the word of God for thousands of years. This will at last give American Israel a firm and lasting spiritual hold in this great country, under the blessings of Providence which has brought us here.[22]

Marshall was won over completely to the cause, expressing both delight and certainty that there would be no problem in finding the additional $25,000.[23] Schiff, however, was away on a trip to the West Indies, and upon his return several weeks later insisted that the library could undoubtedly be had for $100,000, half of which he would be willing to contribute personally. Now, however, he raised a new problem: was the Seminary in a position to take over and properly care for the library?[24]

At a meeting in Solomon Schechter's office a week later, a solution was offered to Schiff's query: the Seminary would house only the 2,000-odd manuscripts from the Gunzburg collection and would ask the New York Public Library to care for the printed books on a temporary basis while the Seminary was erecting new buildings, including an appropriate wing for the library. To clinch the deal with the Gunzburgs, moreover, it was decided that Marx should write to the Baroness immediately to the effect that "a number of gentlemen who are friends of the Seminary" were willing to furnish $100,000 for the library, provided that the proposal was accepted no later than 1 May 1914, and they were assured that they bore no risks should the Russian government interfere with the purchase or export of the library.[25] Marx complied with these instructions, sending a letter to the Baroness with the above terms drafted in precise language by the astute attorney Marshall. Marx decided, however, not to approach the New York Public Library until hearing from St. Petersburg, as he was afraid that in so doing there would be a risk of a leak to the newspapers which might compromise the whole affair.[26]

On 12/25 April 1914, the Baroness wrote a long letter in German to Marx, concluding, *"will ich mich entschliessen das Opfer zu thun, mich von meiner Bibliothek zu trennen. Sie ist viel mehr wert als 200.000 R. aber da es der Wunsch meines seligen Mannes war, die Bibliothek fuer die Gelehrte Jugend offen zu machen, und nicht einzusperren, so glaube ich, dass sie bei Ihrem Seminar am besten zu diesem Zwecke angebracht ist."* She would require that the payment be made in rubles and not dollars, thus avoiding the loss caused by currency exchange, and was certain that the Russian government would not cause any problem—it was not interested in libraries and never forbade any export of books. The Seminary would have to bear the cost of packing and shipping the library, which consisted of all the manuscripts and Hebraica listed in the catalogs she had earlier forwarded. If the Seminary was also interested in the Judaica as well— 2,000 volumes in numerous languages—a separate price would have to be negotiated for that.[27]

When this letter reached New York, Marx immediately sought advice from Marshall and Schiff, and together they composed a reply asserting that the subject matter of all the previous negotiations was the entire library of the late Baron, save works relating to Russian literature—in other words, all the manuscripts and books relating to Hebraica, Semitica, Judaica, and theology in whatever languages they may have been written or printed. Unless this offer was accepted by 1 June 1914, it would be withdrawn.[28]

Certain, at this stage, that the Baroness would agree to all of the Seminary's conditions, Marx met with the chief librarian of the New York Public Library and reached an agreement that the Public Library would house the books that the Seminary could not find room for. In late May, Mathilde Gunzburg fulfilled Marx's expectations, replying that she could not answer all of the Seminary's questions before the deadline, but intended to close the deal as soon as possible.[29] Triumphant, Marx thanked Jacob Schiff for his generosity, for the acquisition of the library would "undoubtedly be of momentous significance for the spiritual development of American Jewry" and was especially symbolic in that "Russia which has up to now sent to our shores the bulk of Jewish immigrants is now yielding up also its most valuable spiritual treasures."[30]

Still, there were various details to clarify: in early June, Marx was informed by the Baroness that a catalog of the books had been completed, listing, in addition to the Hebrew works already counted, 1,500 works in Judaica, 800 in Semitica, and 400 Bible translations in various tongues. The works in "theology," however, were not included. Schiff and Marshall were not perturbed by this lapse, convinced that the deal was now firm; indeed, the latter congratulated Marx "on the position it gives you in the world [as] 'boss' of the greatest Hebraica collection."[31] Together they decided, however, that it would be best for Marx personally to go to St. Petersburg to supervise the packing and shipment of these most valuable wares. Marx was worried that he might not be able to leave America so soon, as his wife was ill, and suggested that if he could not go, Professor Louis Ginzberg ought to take his place. In late June, however, Marx informed Louis Marshall that he was prepared to leave for Russia on July 14 and would apply immediately for a passport and visa.[32]

After a series of frantic cables and notes to and from St. Petersburg in regard to details of the shipment, all major outstanding problems were resolved, and the Baroness wrote to Alexander Marx on 10/23 June 1914 that the sale would include all the manuscripts and books in Hebraica, Judaica, Semitica, Bible translations, and scholarly journals, totaling approximately 14,000 volumes. "I am very pleased to hear that you are coming yourself to St. Petersburg," Baroness Gunzburg concluded, "and my son will be happy to receive you and help you in a foreign town. I am sorry not to be here at that time, for I would have been pleased to receive you in my home."[33]

While Marx was preparing to leave for Russia, he encountered an unexpected obstacle: although he had been in the United States since 1903, he had never become an American citizen, and had only applied for naturalization in March 1914. The State Department therefore refused to issue him a passport, since six months had not elapsed since the first papers were filed, as regulations required. Louis Marshall soon solved this problem by using his political clout to bypass the bureaucracy, but several weeks were lost in the process, and more time was required for Marshall's office to draw up a contract which would satisfy all parties concerned.[34] Finally, on July 21, 1914, the contract— reproduced at the end of this Appendix—was formally signed by Sol M. Stroock, the acting secretary of the Seminary, and was notarized and registered in New York as an official instrument. Alexander Marx then cabled Baroness Gunzburg that the contract was ready and he was awaiting instructions on where it should be sent; three days later the Baroness wired that the contract should be sent to the Hotel Baer in Grindelwald, Switzerland, where she was staying. The contract was thereupon sent from New York to Grindelwald, by registered mail, on 25 July 1914. On the 28th of July, the Baroness wrote once more to Marx thanking him for his help, assuring him that when he arrived in St. Petersburg, her son and secretary would be at his disposal, and expressing the hope that he would take especial care to ensure that the many books in her home not included in the sale would not be tampered with.[35]

On that same day, of course, Austria declared war on Serbia, and within the week, all of Europe was at war, soon to be joined by Japan and Turkey. The fate of the world as a whole hung in the balance. Marx, Schiff, and Marshall quickly realized that the realization of their cherished dream would perforce be postponed by the inaccessibility of both Russia and Germany (where the books were supposed to have been shipped first and the payment deposited in the Warburg Bank), and that new terms might have to be negotiated to arrange the shipment at a later date. On 3 August 1914, Louis Marshall wrote Alexander Marx that since "there has been such a violent change in the history of the world," he had deemed it prudent to cable Baroness Gunzburg as follows: "War necessitates withholding delivery library contract. Further conditions requisite." To Marx, Marshall confessed that

> inasmuch as this cablegram will reach her before our contract does, matters will be left in abeyance. . . . Of course, under existing conditions, it is entirely out of the question that you should go either to Germany or to Russia. In these distracted times you would not be permitted to enter either country, and if you go to Germany you might possibly be called upon to enter the army. Your presence at the Seminary in New York, as a teacher of history, is much more important than your presence in Germany as a maker of history. We must therefore defer the realization of the hope that we have cherished, until after the termination of the present hostilities. In the meantime, let us pray that the library may be preserved from destruction.[36]

Marshall's certainty that the matter was left in abeyance by his cable of August 3 was undermined three months later by the arrival from Switzerland of two letters from Baroness Gunzburg, containing a signed and sealed copy of the contract. On black-bordered paper from the Pension Grande Bretagne in Geneva, the Baroness explained that the copies of the contract sent from New York had finally reached her in mid-October in Geneva, where she was staying due to the death of her father (Baron Ury de Gunzburg, Baron David's uncle). At first she had feared that it was neither prudent nor possible to return the executed contract to New York, but she had been assured by the American consul in Geneva that the boats were going regularly to America and that the agreement would reach the Seminary. Her signature was notarized by the consul himself, and she sent off the contract with the full expectation that it would soon be implemented: "Now I hope the war will soon be finished and that you will be able to come to Petrograd."[37]

Back in New York, the surprised Marx, Schiff, and Marshall conferred on how best to proceed. Schiff counseled that they stand by the offer as far as the price was concerned (it was, after all, his money, and a most substantial sum at that), but that the actual transaction be postponed until after the war. Marshall composed a new letter to the Baroness which would be sent under Marx's name, stating:

> It is with deep regret that I have learned from yours of the 16th ultimo of the great loss which you have sustained through the death of your father, Baron Ury de Gunzburg, and I express my heartfelt sympathy in your bereavement. The trying circumstances accompanying this misfortune are especially sad.
> Shortly after receiving your letter I received a duplicate of the contract between the Seminary and yourself with respect to the collection of books

concerning which we have been negotiating. The contract was forwarded to you to Switzerland for signature. Immediately after the outbreak of the war, and on August 3, 1914, we cabled you as follows: "War necessitates withholding delivery library contract. Further conditions requisite." This you doubtless received, since we have never been informed by the cable company that this message did not reach its destination.

Under the circumstances all matters connected with this arrangement must necessarily remain in abeyance. It will be impossible for me or anybody representing the Seminary to go to Petrograd for the purpose of taking over and supervising the shipment of the library; and for the same reason it is out of the question to make any deposit of money until peace has been restored. It is our intention, whenever it can be safely done, and we are satisfied that the library for which we have negotiated can be acquired and transported here, to carry out the spirit of our understanding, but it may be necessary to make some modifications as to methods and conditions, so that we will receive exactly what we have negotiated for.

I trust that this unfortunate war will soon terminate, so that we may carry out the plans with respect to this library speedily and to the satisfaction of all concerned. [38]

Jacob Schiff, however, was not pleased with this letter: he wrote to Marx on November 16 that "it does not appear to be advisable, under present uncertain conditions as to the time we might be able to get the Gunzburg library—if we shall hereafter be able to get it at all, as it might become destroyed—to re-affirm and continue an engagement made under entirely different conditions and which both the Baroness Gunzburg and we are at this time unable to carry into effect." He therefore insisted that Marx amend the letter drawn up by Marshall by rewriting its ending. Schiff's formulation was as follows:

It is our intention, whenever it can be safely done, and we are satisfied that the library for which we have negotiated can be acquired and transported here, to promptly take up anew the entire proposition as it may be necessary to make some modifications as to methods and conditions, and as no one can now determine how long this terrible war will last and what consequences may follow. [39]

Although Marx realized the significant change implicit in the new wording, at Solomon Schechter's insistence he did not approach Schiff again, and sent the letter off as amended to the Baroness on November 19. She responded, from Geneva, on 4 December 1914.

I just received your letter from November 19 and hasten to answer that the cable you sent me on the 3rd of August never reached me. If I had received it I would not have sent you back one copy of the contract. All the month of August, while everyone was mobilizing, the people were desperate, nobody received letters or telegrams and they were never returned. All was in a horrible confusion. I understand very well that we must wait now till the end of the war and then speak again about the library. I hope it will be soon and send you in the meantime my best regards.[40]

And so the matter rested—until the autumn of 1917, when Alexander Marx heard from colleagues who followed the Russian press that Baroness Gunzburg had sold her husband's library to the Russian Zionists for 500,000 rubles. Marx passed on this news to Cyrus Adler, the acting president of the Seminary after Schechter's death, who asked Marx to determine the status of the contract with the Baroness. Louis Marshall advised Marx that given the fall in the value of the Russian currency, half a million rubles was probably worth less than the $100,000 agreed to by the Seminary; he was, in fact, scheduled to meet with one of the young Barons Gunzburg in Washington in a few days, and if he was given any further facts, he would try to "induce the Baroness Gunzburg to keep her contract with us." More important, it was his legal opinion that

> that contract is still in force. It has never been cancelled. Its performance was prevented by the outbreak of the war. It has always been our idea that as soon as it was possible for you to go to Petrograd to take over the books, it would be carried out on our part. It is certainly most extraordinary that the Baroness should have undertaken to sell the books to the Zionists when there was still an outstanding contract to sell them to the Seminary.[41]

Marx answered a few days later that he had just heard that the amount contracted for by the Zionists had not yet been fully raised, and that of the 500,000 rubles, the Baroness herself was to contribute 100,000. He thought it an excellent idea that Marshall meet with the young Baron, but did not agree with Marshall on the legal issue: on the contrary, he believed that legally the Baroness was not bound to her agreement with the Seminary, because from her letter of December 4, 1914, she seemed to have understood the Seminary's letter of the previous November 19 to mean a cancellation of the contract, and this seems also to have been the intention of Schiff's letter of November 16.[42] Marx repeated the same conclusion in a memorandum he sent to Cyrus Adler regarding the Gunzburg library on 3 October 1917. With this memorandum, the Seminary's files on the subject come to an end.[43]

Had the sale of the collection to the Russian Zionists for the Hebrew University been carried out, it is not at all certain whether Alexander Marx's amateur legal opinion would have been outweighed by Louis Marshall's legal expertise and dexterity in litigation. Of course, the case was never put to the test, due to the Soviet regime's refusal to allow the materials to leave Russia.

But the story of the connection between the Jewish Theological

Seminary and the Gunzburg library does not end in 1917. Apparently, in the mid-1930s, representatives of the Soviet government made some overtures to the Seminary in regard to the Gunzburg materials. Thus, on 12 July 1935, Cyrus Adler wrote to Felix Warburg:

> I fear the Russians' bringing presents. I doubt the sincerity of the statement that they have great pride in the Ginzburg [*sic*] Library and insist upon keeping it as though it were a national monument. How can anybody explain their willingness to sell the Sinaiticus to the British Museum for $500,000 and get so terribly excited about the Hebrew manuscripts and books of Baron Ginzburg [*sic*], most of which are in the Hebrew language, which is banned in Russia. I should have to have much more concrete evidence of good faith on their part before taking up either with the Academy of Sciences at Moscow or at Leningrad the question of appointing a research man, etc. etc. . . .
>
> Now as far as [Judah L.] Magnes is concerned on this point, and I am not taking up anything else, the collection belongs to the Hebrew University. It was bought for the University and paid for, and was seized by the Soviet Government. It ought to be released by the Soviet Government to the University. It is in no sense a Russian national monument. The Soviet Government, in taking this step, has done what no other government, civilized or uncivilized, has ever done to my knowledge, namely, to take a private collection which had no relation to the country in which it was, consisting of books and manuscripts entirely from other places, and seized in my opinion merely as a matter of loot, and possibly because of the early Soviet rage against the nationalism in Palestine. . . . [44]

Exactly what "presents" the Russians were offering the Seminary is not clear from this letter, and unfortunately the Adler archives contain no further information on this matter. Until and unless further materials come to light, this tantalizing hint of a final chapter in the history of the sale of the Gunzburg library to the Jewish Theological Seminary—like many other facets of the fate of the Gunzburg collection after the October Revolution—must remain mired in mystery.

APPENDIX[45]

AGREEMENT made and entered into this twenty-first day of July, 1914, between BARONESS MATHILDE DE GÜNZBURG, of St. Petersburg, Russia, hereinafter called the Vendor, and THE JEWISH THEOLOGICAL SEMINARY of AMERICA,—hereinafter called the Purchaser.

FIRST: The Vendor hereby sells, and the Purchaser buys, upon the terms hereinafter set forth, the entire collection of manuscripts, pamphlets and books forming the library of the late Baron David de Gunzburg, consisting of Hebraica, Semitica, and Judaica, theological works in various languages, excluding only books not referring to Jewish or Semitic history or science; the intention of the parties hereto being to include in the sale hereby evinced all works, whether in manuscript or printed, and whether in Hebrew or in any other language, which in any way relate to Jews or Semitic literature, philosophy or science or history, or which are of Jewish interest, in theology in character or subject-matter, whether included in any catalogue prepared by and for the Vendor or not, and which during his lifetime belonged or appertained to the aforesaid library of the late Baron David de Gunzburg. Any dispute with regard to the classification of any such books or manuscripts shall be decided by the agent of the Purchaser hereinafter mentioned, and his decision shall be conclusive.

SECOND: The Purchaser agrees to pay, and the Vendor agrees to accept, as and for the full purchase price of the library, the sum of two hundred thousand (200,000) rubles, to be paid as follows: The full sum of two hundred thousand (200,000) rubles shall, within ten (10) days after the return to the Purchaser in New York of a duplicate original of this agreement, duly executed and acknowledged by the Vendor, be deposited with the banking house of M. M. Warburg of Hamburg, Germany, to be paid to the Vendor in the following manner: The Purchaser's agent shall proceed to St. Petersburg, and examine, pack and ship (for which every facility shall be afforded him by the Vendor) the entire collection hereby sold, for which a receipt, expressing in general terms the Vendor's compliance with this contract, shall be given her by the Purchaser's agent. Upon presentation and surrender of said receipt to the bankers, the said sum of two hundred thousand (200,000) rubles shall at once be paid to the Vendor. The Vendor agrees that any shortage, owing to error in making delivery to the Purchaser's agent at St. Petersburg, will be immediately rectified by her.

THIRD: The Purchaser agrees to bear the entire expense of packing and shipping said library, and all the risk of loss after said library shall have been delivered to St. Petersburg, except that in the event of interference by the Government authority, preventing delivery of said library in New York, this contract shall terminate, and both parties be relieved from the obligations thereof, and the sum of two hundred thousand (200,000) rubles deposited as aforesaid by the Purchaser shall be returned to it by said bankers, or by the Vendor if she shall have received said sum.

FOURTH: The Purchaser hereby appoints Professor Alexander Marx and Professor Louis Ginzberg, of New York City, New York, agents for the purpose of this agreement, with full authority to both or either of them to represent it with respect to any and all matters pertaining to this contract, and to perform any act, or execute in the name of the Purchaser any certificate, receipt or other instrument requisite, useful or proper to carry out the purpose and intent of this instrument or any of its provisions and covenants.

FIFTH: The Vendor does hereby, for herself, her heirs, executors and administrators, covenant that she is the sole owner of, and has good right to sell and transfer, the said library and every part thereof, and that she will warrant and defend the title of the said library hereby sold unto the said Purchaser, its successors _____ and consigns, against all and every person and persons whomsoever, and any and all claims, demands, liens and encumbrances whatsoever.

SIXTH: The Purchaser hereby covenants that the said library, so long as owned by the Purchaser, shall be known and designated as the "Baron David de Gunzburg Collection," or by such other appropriate name as shall be approved by the Vendor.

IN WITNESS WHEREOF, the parties have hereunto set their hands and applied their seals, the said Vendor at Geneva, Switzerland on the 23rd day of October 1914, and the said Purchaser at New York City, New York, on the 21st day of July 1914.

(signed) Baroness Mathilde de Gunzburg

Witness
Francis P. J. Keene

THE JEWISH THEOLOGICAL SEMINARY OF AMERICA

(signed) By Sol M. Stroock
Acting Secretary

Witness as to
Sol M. Stroock
Emma R. Dennis

Confederation of Switzerland   )   )
City and Canton of Geneva   ),s.s. : ss.:
Consulate of the United States of America)   )

BE IT REMEMBERED, that, on this 23rd day of October in the year one thousand nine hundred and fourteen, before me, the undersigned, Consul of the United States of America at Geneva, Switzerland, personally appeared Baroness Mathilde de Gunzburg, to me known, and known to me to be the individual described in and who executed the foregoing instrument, and she duly acknowledged to me that she executed the same.

IN TEST WHEREOF, I have hereunto subscribed my name and affixed my official seal at Geneva, Switzerland, the day and the year last aforesaid.

(signed) Francis P. J. Keene
Consul of the United States of America
Geneva, Switzerland

United States of America)
State of New York   : ss:
County of New York   )

On this 21st day of July, in the year one thousand nine hundred and fourteen, before me personally came SOL M. STROOCK to me known, who, being by me duly sworn, did depose and say, that he resides in the Borough of Manhattan, City of New York, State of New York; that he is the Acting Secretary of the JEWISH THEOLOGICAL SEMINARY of AMERICA, the corporation described in and which executed the foregoing instrument; that he knows the corporation seal of said corporation; that the seal affixed to said instrument is such corporate seal, and that it was so affixed by order of the Board of Trustees of said corporation, and that he signed his name hereunto by like order.

(signed) Emma R. Dennis
Notary Public, Westchester Co.
Certificate filed in New York Co. No. 33
New York Register's No. 6077
Bronx Co. No. 38, Bronx
Register's No. 611

NOTES

I should like to thank Dr. Menachem Schmelzer, librarian of the Jewish Theological Seminary of America, for his assistance and advice during the researching of this article, and for permission to publish the archival material cited herein. I am also grateful to Chancellor Gerson D. Cohen for sharing with me *torah she-be'al peh* on this matter.

1. There is as yet no reliable scholarly work on the Gunzburg family. The most substantive information can be gleaned, inter alia, from the following works: *Evreiskaia entsiklopediia* (St. Petersburg, n.d.), vol. 6, 525–534, entries by G. Sliozberg, Iu. Gessen, and G. Genkel; Henri Sliosberg, *Baron Horace O. de Gunzbourg, sa vie et son oeuvre* (Paris, 1935); David Maggid, *Sefer toledot mishpahat Gintsburg* (St. Petersburg, 1899), pp 79–80, 140, 154–155, 206–207, 251–258; Shaul Ginsburg, "Di familie Baron Gintsburg: drei doyres shtadlones, tsedoke, un haskole," in his *Historishe Verk* (New York, 1937), vol. 2, pp. 117–159; Sh. L. Tsitron, *Shtadlonim* (Warsaw, n.d.), 334–376. On Baron David Gunzburg, especially see the collection of memoirs and articles published on the occasion of the centennial of his birth in *He-'Avar* 6 (1958): 75–178, and the often caustic comments of Simon Dubnov in his memoirs, *Kniga zhizni* (Riga, 1934–35), vols. 1 and 2, index. On the Gunzburg library, see *Evreiskaia entsiklopediia*, vol. 4, s.v. "Biblioteki v Rossii," the various memoirs already cited, and most recently, Mordekhai Nadav, "Le-toledot ha-ma'amazim le-rekhishat 'osef David Ginzburg beshvil beit-ha-sefarim ha-le'umi be-Yerushalayim," in *Essays and Studies in Librarianship Presented to Curt David Wormann on his 75th Birthday* (Jerusalem, 1975), pp. 81–95.

2. Mordekhai Nadav, article cited in n.1. There, Nadav noted that a second installment on the subject, concerning the later years, will be published at a later date. This second article, unfortunately, has not appeared at the time of the conclusion of this essay.

3. See, for now, in addition to the sources cited in Nadav: Sh. Eisenstadt, "Megillat sefer," *Ha-'Olam* 23 (1935): 320–321 and 336–337; the various redactions, descriptions, and comments referring to the Gunzburg collection in Abraham I. Katsh, *Catalogue of Hebrew Manuscripts Preserved in the USSR (Acquired on Microfilm)*, 2 vols. (New York, 1957); idem, *Ginze mishnah* (Jerusalem, 1970); and idem, "Hebrew and Judeo-Arabic MSS in the Collections of the USSR," in *Trudy dvatsat-piatogo Mezhdunarodnogo kongressa vostokovedov, Moskva 9–16 avgusta 1960* (Moscow, 1962), vol. 1, pp. 421–429. For cautionary comments on Katsh's works, see Patricia K. Grimsted, *Archives and Manuscript Repositories in the U.S.S.R., Supplement 1, Bibliographical Addenda* (Zug, Switzerland, 1976), p.13.

4. Ginsburg, "Di familie Baron Gintsburg," p. 159.

5. These documents are contained in the Archives of the Jewish Theological Seminary of America, New York, under accession number 3–8, Box 5. Approximately 110 of the documents were acquired in 1978 from Mr. James Marshall, son of Louis Marshall, and were interfiled with the Seminary library's own files on the affair already held in the archives. Photocopies of the Marshall materials were sent to the American Jewish Archives in Cincinnati to be added there to the Louis Marshall papers. Since the files in Box 5 are not numbered, in the references to follow, I shall cite documents and letters by the name of the file, the author and correspondent, and the date of the document.

6. File 1911–1913, Israel Friedlaender to Jacob Schiff, 11 January 1911.

7. Ibid.

8. Ibid.

9. File 1911–1913, Jacob Schiff to Israel Friedlaender, 12 January 1911.

10. File 1911–1913, Samuel Wiener to Alexander Marx, 3/16 February 1911. According to Zalman Shazar, Wiener was bitterly disappointed that the Baron asked him merely to teach Jewish bibliography at the "Higher Courses on Oriental Studies" rather than appoint him lecturer in Hebrew literature. Gunzburg was supposed to have quipped that Wiener was the greatest expert on Hebrew title-pages, but not on the content of the works. See Shazar's memoir on the Baron and his school in the above-cited *He-'Avar* 6 (1958), 90.

11. File 1911–1913, Zalman Amitan to Alexander Marx, 28 January/9 February 1911, 14/27 February 1911, 25 February/10 March 1911.

12. File 1911–1913, Mayer Sulzberger to Alexander Marx, 12 March 1911.

13. File 1911–1913, Jacob Schiff to Alexander Marx, 17 March 1911.

14. File 1911–1913, Felix Warburg to Baron Alexander Gunzburg, 1 May 1912; on the catalog, see Alexander Marx to Jacob Schiff, 24 March 1913.

15. File 1911–1913, Alexander Marx to Louis Marshall, 31 December 1912.

16. File 1911–1913, Alexander Marx to Baroness Gunzburg, 19 March 1913

17. File 1911–1913, Baroness Gunzburg to Alexander Marx, 4 April 1913.

18. File 1911–1913, Alexander Marx to Baroness Gunzburg, 15 April 1913.

19. File March–April 1914, Alexander Marx to Louis Marshall, 20 March 1914.

20. File March–April 1914, Baroness Gunzburg to Alexander Marx, 23 February/8 March 1914.

21. File March–April 1914, Solomon Schechter to Louis Marshall, 20 March 1914.

22. File March–April 1914, Solomon Schechter to Jacob Schiff, 20 March 1914.

23. File March–April 1914, Louis Marshall to Alexander Marx, 21 March 1914.

24. File March–April 1914, Jacob Schiff to Alexander Marx, 2 April 1914.

25. File March–April 1914, Louis Marshall to Alexander Marx, 11 April 1914.

26. File March–April 1914, Alexander Marx to Louis Marshall, 13 April 1914.

27. File March–April 1914, Baroness Gunzburg to Alexander Marx, 12/25 April 1914.

28. File May 1914, Alexander Marx to Baroness Gunzburg, 11 May 1914.

29. File May 1914, Baroness Gunzburg to Alexander Marx, 8/21 May 1914.

30. File June 1–17, 1914, Alexander Marx to Jacob Schiff, 3 June 1914.

31. File June 1–17, 1914, Louis Marshall to Alexander Marx, 7 June 1914.

32. File June 18–30, 1914, Alexander Marx to Jacob Schiff, 21 June 1914.

33. File June 18–30, 1914, Baroness Gunzburg to Alexander Marx, 10/23 June 1914.

34. See the series of letters between Alexander Marx, Jacob Schiff, Louis Marshall, and Marshall's junior colleague Abraham Benedict in File June 18–30, 1914, and File July 1–15, 1914, culminating in the letter from Abraham Benedict to Alexander Marx, 13 July 1914.

35. File July 16–30, 1914, Baroness Gunzburg to Alexander Marx, 28 July 1914.

36. File August 1914, Louis Marshall to Alexander Marx, 3 August 1914.

37. File October–December 1914, Baroness Gunzburg to Alexander Marx, 16 October 1914 and 23 October 1914.

38. File October–December 1914, Louis Marshall to Alexander Marx, 13 November 1914.

39. File October–December 1914, Jacob Schiff to Alexander Marx, 16 November 1914.

40. File October–December 1914, Baroness Gunzburg to Alexander Marx, 4 December 1914.

41. File September–November 1917, Louis Marshall to Alexander Marx, 29 September 1917.

42. File September–November 1917, Alexander Marx to Louis Marshall, 3 October 1917.

43. File September–November 1917, Alexander Marx to Cyrus Adler, 3 October 1917.

44. Ira Robinson, ed., *Cyrus Adler: Selected Letters* (Philadelphia, 1985), vol. II, p. 303. See also Adler's letter to Alexander Marx on 5 September 1919, vol. I, p. 390.

45. File "Agreement between Baroness Mathilde de Guenzburg and the Jewish Theological Seminary of America, July 21, 1914." This file contains the original contract forwarded to the Baroness, and three copies of this agreement held in New York, as well as two copies of an earlier version of the contract amended by hand.

Appendix B

**DISTRIBUTION OF HEIRLESS CULTURAL PROPERTY:
OFFENBACH ARCHIVAL
DEPOT, JEWISH CULTURAL
RECONSTRUCTION FOUNDATION**

Table 1
OFFENBACH ARCHIVAL DEPOT DISPOSITION OF MATERIALS
MARCH 2, 1946–APRIL 30, 1949

Outgoing Shipments	*No. of Items*
France	377,204
Netherlands	334,241
Union of Soviet Socialist Republics	273,645
Italy	252,068
Austria	51,305
Poland	34,362
Czechoslovakia	14,587
Greece	8,511
Great Britain	5,443
Belgium	5,332
Yugoslavia	3,664
Norway	1,074
Switzerland	637
Hungary	423
U.S. Zone of Occupation	1,380,552
Yiddish Scientific Institute (YIVO)	79,951
Jewish Cultural Reconstruction Committee	77,603

Library of Congress Mission........................	20,329
British Zone of Occupation.........................	10,796
In Storage..	161,681
Ready for Shipment	85,167
In Processing	26,623
Total......................................	3,205,198

SOURCE: Monthly reports of the Offenbach Archival Depot.

Table 2

OFFENBACH ARCHIVAL DEPOT DISPOSITION OF MATERIALS WITHIN THE
UNITED STATES ZONE OF OCCUPATION
MARCH 2, 1946–APRIL 30, 1949

Disposition	No. of Items
Preussische Staatsbibliothek, Berlin	700,000
Baileeship of Minister President of *Land* Hesse	296,473
Bipartite Finance Board, Bad Homburg	190,843
Stadt- und Universitaetsbibliothek Frankfurt................	79,310
Grosse Nationale Mutterloge zu den 3 Weltkugeln	49,853
American Joint Distribution Committee	20,923
Wiesbaden Central Collecting Point....................	17,279
Board of Education and Culture for the Liberated Jews in Germany	6,000
G-2 Division OMGUS	5,957
Finance Division OMGUS...........................	4,361
Hesse Regional Library, Darmstadt....................	3,000
St. George's Seminary, Frankfurt	1,799
Munich Central Collecting Point	1,690
Wuerttembergische Landesbibliothek, Stuttgart................	1,544
Miscellaneous......................................	1,520
Total......................................	1,380,552

SOURCE: Monthly reports of the Offenbach Archival Depot.

JEWISH CULTURAL RECONSTRUCTION, INC.

DISTRIBUTION OF BOOKS FROM NEW YORK DEPOT
JULY 1, 1949–NOV. 30, 1950

According to Institutions

Name of Institution	No. Rec'd	No. Ret'ned	Net Rec'd
A. *Priority Libraries*			
1. American Jewish Historical Soc'ty	43		43
2. Baltimore Hebrew College	1,887	3	1,884
3. Brandeis University	2,569		2,569
4. College of Jew. Studies, Chicago	3,561		3,561
5. Dropsie College	3,475	465	3,010
6. Hebrew Teachers College, Boston	1,958		1,958
7. Hebrew Theol. College, Chicago	3,020	99	2,921
8. Hebrew Union College, Cincinnati	2,388	67	2,321
9. Jewish Community Library, L.A.	907		907
10. Jewish Institute of Religion	6,409	1,036	5,373
11. Jewish Theological Seminary	4,445	45	4,400
12. Mesifta Chaim Berlin	1,105		1,105
13. Mesifta Torah Vodaath	3,713		3,713
14. Ner Israel, Baltimore	2,582		2,582
15. Rabbinical College of Telshe	156		156
16. Yeshiva University (Including 5,932 of Stuermer Collection)	8,429	350	8,079
17. Yiddish Scientific Institute	3,379	89	3,290
B. *Smaller Libraries*			
1. B'nai Brith Hillel Foundation	1,013	448	565
2. Beth Medrash Elyon	350		350
3. Beth Medrash Govoha	450		450
4. Jewish Teachers Seminary	615		615
5. Jewish Welfare Board	200		200
6. Mirrer Yeshiva	400		400
7. Schneersohn Library	990		990
8. Yeshiva of Flatbush	332		332
9. Zionist Archives	970		970
C. *Non-Jewish Libraries*			
1. Columbia University	69		69
2. City College	214		214
3. Harvard University	200	65	135
4. Johns Hopkins University	2		2

5. Library of Congress	2,372		2,372
6. New York Public Library	104		104
7. New York University	224		224
8. University of Texas	635		635
9. Yale University	387		387

D. *One Time Allocations*

Yeshivoth (through Torah Umesorah)	12,013	254	11,759
Hebrew Convalescent Home	182		182
Jewish Settlement House	28		28

E. *Abroad*

Canada	3,149	3,149
Hebrew University Library	4,400	4,400
Bibliothèque Nationale via Alliance Israélite Universelle	17	17

F. *Individual Claimants*

	315		315
Total Distributed	79,657	2,921	76,736

G. *Closed Cases*

Individual Claimants	16 Cases
HUL	19 Cases of Periodicals

ACCORDING TO CATEGORIES

Category	No. of Books
Rabbinics	19,336
Bible	550
Ritual	1,382
Biur	1,028
Kabbalah	385
Modern Religious Literature	2,603
Fiction (Yiddish and Hebrew)	3,014
Secular Literature	8,827
German Judaica	8,802
Post-revolutionary Russian Literature	2,522
German Jewish Periodicals	24,143
Schoolbooks and Miscellaneous	644
Stuermer Collection	5,932
Miscellaneous (including 79 books individual claimants)	489
Total	79,657

NOTE: All periodicals, whether individual issues or bound volumes, were counted as single items. Some of the figures are therefore misleading as to the actual number of titles.

MEMORANDUM

TO: The Members of the Board of Directors and the
    Advisory Committee
FROM: Hannah Arendt, Executive Secretary

August 18, 1950

Re: Distribution of Ceremonial Objects, New York Depot

1,698 out of a total of about 3,800 ceremonial objects, in the category of
museum pieces, have been allocated and are ready for shipment.

Schedule A: List of Institutions and Number of Objects

1. The Jewish Museum	127	Items
2. Hebrew Teachers College, Roxbury, Mass.	53	"
3. B'nai Brith Hillel Foundations, N.Y.C.	65	"
4. Hebrew Theological College, Chicago	53	"
5. College of Jewish Studies, Chicago	56	"
6. New York University, Library of Judaica and Hebraica, N.Y.C.	36	"
7. Brooklyn Museum, Brooklyn	19	"
8. Museum of Hebrew Union College, Cincinnati	99	"
9. The Temple, Cleveland, Ohio	70	"
10. Yeshiva University, N.Y.C.	245	"
11. National Jewish Welfare Board, N.Y.C.	147	"
12. Committee on Restoration of Continental Jewish Museums, Libraries and Archives, London, England	247	"
13. So. African Jewish Board of Deputies, Johannesburg, So. Africa	150	"
14. Canadian Jewish Congress, Montreal, Canada	151	"
15. Delagacion de Asociasiones Israelitas Argentinas, Buenos Aires, Argentina	150	"
16. Joods Hulp-Comite Curacao, Curacao, N.W. Indies	30	"
Total	1,698	Items

Schedule B: Categories of Distributed Items

Eternal Lights	4
Torah Shields	212
Pointers	196
Spice Boxes	274
Cups	64

Plates	53
Menoroth	133
Hanukah Lamps	182
Collecting Boxes	20
Rimonim	180
Textiles (Torah Curtains, etc.)	96
Torah Wrappers	100
Ataroth Ornaments	88
Megiloth	9
Candlesticks	12
Torah Crowns	17
Medals and Coins	35
Miscellaneous	23
Total	1,698 Items

Appendix C

Library Statistics
July 1, 1985–June 30, 1986

Technical Services

Number of titles acquired	2,449
Number of volumes acquired	3,265
Number of titles cataloged....................	3,954
Number of volumes processed	5,789

Public Services

Number of volumes borrowed	15,935
Number of library visitors....................	95,613
Interlibrary loan—Borrowed..................	83
Interlibrary loan—Loaned....................	222

Staff (as of June 30, 1986)

Professional—Full-time	8
—Part-time	3 (1.8 FTE)
—Full-time equivalent	9.8
Other professional—Full-time...................	3
—Part-time.................	3 (1.4 FTE)
—Full-time equivalent..........	4.4
Support Staff—Full-time	9
—Part-time	2 (1.0 FTE)
—Full-time equivalent.............	10

Totals—Full-time.............................   20
    —Part-time.............................   8
    —Full-time equivalent 24.2

General Data

Number of titles in library   218,965
Number of volumes in library   273,911
Number of volumes cataloged (10/66–6/86)......   149,297
Periodical subscriptions   700
Number of microforms   11,000
Number of rare books   15,000
Number of manuscripts......................   11,100

Physical plant

55,000 square feet
500,000 volumes shelf capacity
300 seating capacity

Notes

CHAPTER ONE

1. Moshe Davis, *The Emergence of Conservative Judaism* (New York, 1963).
2. Ibid., pp. 177 f.
3. Ibid., p. 226.
4. *Proceedings of the First Biennial Convention of the Jewish Theological Seminary Association* (New York, 1888), p. 9.
5. Ibid., p. 18.
6. Naomi Cohen, *Encounter with Emancipation* (Philadelphia, 1984), pp. 180 f.
7. Quoted from his *Ethics of the Fathers*, as cited by Cohen, p. 181.
8. Ibid., p. 18.
9. See Joshua Bloch, *Of Making Many Books: An Annotated List of the Books Issued by the Jewish Publication Society of America, 1890–1952.*
10. For literature on Adler, see: Cyrus Adler, *I Have Considered the Days*, (Philadelphia, 1945); Herbert Parzen, *Architects of Conservative Judaism* (New York, 1964); Cyrus Adler, *Selected Letters*, ed. Ira Robinson, 2 vols., (Philadelphia and New York, 1985); David G. Dalin, "Cyrus Adler, Non-Zionism, and the Zionist Movement: A Study in Contradictions," *AJS Review* 10, no 1, (Spring 1985): 55 f.
11. See *Addresses Delivered in Memory of Mayer Sulzberger* (Philadelphia, 1924); Alexander Marx, *Essays in Jewish Biography* (Philadelphia, 1947), pp. 223 f.; Davis, *Emergence of Conservative Judaism*, 362 f.
12. See Norman Bentwich, *Solomon Schechter: A Biography* (New York, 1938); his writings are assembled in Adolph S. Oko, *Solomon Schechter: A Bibliography* (Cambridge, 1938).
13. Bentwich, *Solomon Schechter*, p. 124.
14. See Abraham J. Karp, "Solomon Schechter Comes to America," *American Jewish Historical Quarterly* 53, nos. 1–4 (September 1963): 42 ff.
15. See Meir Ben-Horin, "Solomon Schechter to Judge Mayer Sulzberger," Part I: "Letters from the Pre-Seminary Period (1895–1901)," *Jewish Social Studies*, 25, no. 4 (October 1963): 249 f.; Part II: "Letters from the Seminary Period (1902–1915)," ibid., 27, no. 2, (April 1965): 75 f.; Supplement to Parts I and II, ibid. 30, no. 4 (October 1968): 262 f.
16. Ibid., pt. I, p. 261.
17. Ibid., p. 257.
18. Ibid., p. 256. At this stage, the terms "Orthodox" and "Conservative" are synonymous with "Traditional." On the history of both as identifying movements, see

Davis, *Emergence of Conservative Judaism*, pp. 311 f.; Robert Gordis, *Understanding Conservative Judaism* (New York, 1978), pp. 3 f.; Jeffrey S. Gurock, "Resisters and Accommodators: Varieties of Orthodox Rabbis in America 1886–1983," *American Jewish Archives* 25, no. 2 (November 1983): 100 f.; Abraham J. Karp, "The Conservative Rabbi—Dissatisfied, But Not Unhappy," ibid., pp. 188 ff.

19. Ben-Horin, "Solomon Schechter to Judge Mayer Sulzberger," pt. I, pp. 260 f.
20. Ibid., p. 262.
21. Ibid.
22. Ibid., p. 261.
23. Ibid., p. 265.
24. Ibid., p. 275.
25. Ibid.
26. Ibid., p. 277.
27. Ibid., p. 272. Schiff, a descendant of a traditional family from Frankfurt-Main, Germany, observed ritual laws and practices throughout his life. See Cyrus Adler, *Jacob Schiff: His Life and Letters* (New York, 1928), 1:3 f., 2:44 f.
28. Adler, *Selected Letters*, I:90 f.
29. Ibid., p. 92.
30. For details, see the *Biennial Report of the Jewish Theological Seminary, 1902–1904* (New York, 1906).
31. Introduction to *Seminary Addresses and Other Papers by Solomon Schechter* (New York, 1959), p. xi.
32. Eli Ginzberg, *Keeper of the Law: Louis Ginzberg* (Philadelphia, 1966), pp. 61 f.
33. Ben-Horin, "Solomon Schechter to Judge Mayer Sulzberger," pt. II, p. 77.
34. *JTS Biennial Report, 1902–1904*, p. 74.
35. *United Synagogue Recorder*, vol. 5., no 1, pp. 11 f.
36. Copy of telegram in JTS Archives. The original, dated July 7, 1903, reads: "*Falls Ihr Seminar unabaenderlich fest auf tradirter Grundlage steht und nur in Ihrem Sinne lehrt, habe gegen Alexanders Eintritt nichts einzuwenden.*"
37. Exchange of letters between Schechter and Davidson of May 18 and 21, 1905 (JTS Archives).
38. See Ben-Horin, "Solomon Schechter to Judge Mayer Sulzberger," pt. II, p. 76, and Gurock, "Resisters and Accommodators," pp. 106 f.
39. *JTS Biennial Report, 1902–1904*, pp. 102 f.
40. *Seminary Addresses*, pp. 48 f.
41. *JTS Biennial Report, 1902–1904*, pp. 117 f.

CHAPTER TWO

1. Meir Ben-Horin, "Solomon Schechter to Judge Mayer Sulzberger," Part I, "Letters from the Pre-Seminary Period (1895–1901)," *Jewish Social Studies* 25, no. 4 (October 1963): 286.
2. Schechter Archives, JTS.
3. *Biennial Report of the Jewish Theological Seminary, 1902–1904* (New York, 1906), pp. 49 ff.
4. S. Berkowitz, "Ephraim Deinard: Bibliophile and Bookman," *Studies in Bibliography and Booklore* 9 (1971): 137 f.; Jacob Kabakoff, *Shocharim Ve' Ne'emanim* (Jerusalem, 1978), pp. 20 f.
5. Ephraim Deinard, *Or Meir: Catalogue of the Old Hebrew Manuscripts and Printed Books of the Library of Hon. M. Sulzberger of Philadelphia, Pa.* (New York, 1896).
6. Ibid., p. 57 n. 26.
7. Marx's doctoral dissertation, *Seder Olam Rabbah*, completed a few years later, in

1903, included material obtained during his visit to Schechter, to whom he pays great tribute.

8. *Seminary Addresses and other Papers by Solomon Schechter* (New York, 1959), pp. 119 f.; Alexander Marx, "Moritz Steinschneider," *Studies in Jewish History and Booklore* (New York 1944), pp. 364 f.

9. The work, written in Latin, is entitled *Catalogus Librorum Hebraeorum in Bibliotheca Bodleiana* (Berlin, 1852–60).

10. *Seminary Addresses*, pp. 17 f.

11. Ibid., "Beginnings of Jewish *Wissenschaft*," p. 173.

12. On Hoffmann, see Marx's essay in his *Studies in Jewish History and Booklore*, pp. 369 f.

13. Letter, JTS Marx Archives.

14. Ibid.

15. Annual report from September 1903 to September 1904, JTS Archives.

16. JTS Marx Archives.

17. Letter, ibid.

18. George Alexander Kohut, "Steinschneideriana," in *Studies in Jewish Bibliography and Related Subjects in Memory of Abraham Solomon Freidus* (New York, 1929), pp. 68, 85.

19. Letter, JTS Marx Archives.

20. Letter Schiff, September 14, 1898, JTS Marx Archives.

21. Of this ambitious undertaking, only one volume appeared in 1925, entitled: *Gesammelte Schriften* I, ed. Heinrich Malter and Alexander Marx (Berlin, 1925). The plan was to include Steinschneider's copious notes, written in very small handwriting, with his essays.

22. See Boaz Cohen, "Bibliography of the Works of Professor Alexander Marx," *United Synagogue Recorder*, 8, no. 1 (February 1928): 86, 87, 194, 195.

23. Marx, "The Library," *The Jewish Theological Seminary of America Semicentennial Volume* (New York, 1939), p. 95.

24. *Seminary Addresses*, "The Emancipation of Jewish Science," pp. 3 f.

25. Schechter, "The Study of the Bible," *Studies in Judaism*, Second Series (Philadelphia, 1908), pp. 40 f.

26. *Seminary Addresses*, pp. 35 f.

27. Meir Ben-Horin, "Solomon Schechter to Judge Mayer Sulzberger," Part II, "Letters from the Seminary Period (1902–1915)," *Jewish Social Studies* 27, no. 2 (April 1965): 81 f. Letter of Rabbi Max Heller, Temple Sinai, New Orleans, October 31, 1904.

28. Schechter was probably referring to the *Union Prayer Book*, which he labeled "an abomination." Ben Horin, "Solomon Schechter to Judge Meyer Sulzberger," pt. II, p. 94.

29. Ibid., p. 83.

30. Ibid., p. 97.

31. Ibid., p. 98. For a detailed account, see Michael Stanislawski's "An Unperformed Contract: The Sale of Baron Gunzburg's Library to the Jewish Theological Seminary of America," Appendix A.

32. Letter, JTS Schiff Archives.

33. *Seminary Addresses*, pp. xxiii f. and 91 f.; see also Cyrus Adler, *Jacob H. Schiff: His Life and Letters* (New York, 1928), 2:165 f. and Norman Bentwich *Solomon Schechter: A Biography* (New York, 1938), pp. 320 f.

34. Bentwich, *Solomon Schechter*, p. 215.

35. *Seminary Addresses*, p. 88.

36. Bentwich, *Solomon Schechter*, pp. 187 f.

37. Ben-Horin, "Solomon Schechter to Judge Mayer Sulzberger" pt. II, p. 94; see also a previous letter in which Schechter called Levinthal "an ambitious Jesuit," ibid., p. 80.

38. Herbert Rosenblum, *Conservative Judaism* (New York 1983), p. 18.

39. Cyrus Adler, *Selected Letters*, ed. Ira Robinson, 2 vols. (Philadelphia and New York, 1985), I:204 f.

40. Herbert Parzen, *Architects of Conservative Judaism* (New York, 1964), p. 69.

41. Bentwich, *Solomon Schechter*, p. 224.

42. *Seminary Addresses*, pp. 229 f.

CHAPTER THREE

1. Eli Ginzberg, *Keeper of the Law: Louis Ginzberg* (Philadelphia, 1966), p. 132.

2. Herbert Parzen, *Architects of Conservative Judaism* (New York, 1964), pp. 178 f.

3. Ibid., p. 94.

4. Exchange of letters between Marshall and Mathilde Schechter of December 28 and 30, 1915. JTS Marshall Archives.

5. Louis Ginzberg, *Ginze Schechter*, 2 vols. (Jerusalem, 1928).

6. Israel Davidson, *Ginze Schechter* (Jerusalem, 1928).

7. On this life and works, see Baila Round Shargel, *Practical Dreamer: Israel Friedlaender and the Shaping of American Judaism* (New York, 1986).

8. Marx, "The Library," *The Jewish Theological Seminary of America: Semicentennial Volume* (New York, 1939), pp. 96 f.

9. For a more detailed description, see Alexander Marx, "The Seminary Library's Great Accession, The Elkan N. Adler Collection." *United Synagogue Recorder* 3, no. 2 (April 1923): 6 f., and idem, "The Library," pp. 97 f.

10. Elkan Nathan Adler, *About Hebrew Manuscripts* (London, 1905); *Catalogue of Hebrew Manuscripts in the Collection of E. N. Adler* (Cambridge University Press, 1921).

11. Cyrus Adler, *Selected Lettters*, ed. Ira Robinson, 2 vols. (Philadelphia and New York, 1985), 1:390.

12. Ibid. II: pp 56 f.

13. At the time a pound was worth $4.20.

14. Samuel E. Karff, ed., *Hebrew Union College–Jewish Institute of Religion at One Hundred Years* (Hebrew Union College Press, 1976), p. 73.

15. Adler, *Selected Letters*, II:65 f.

16. JTS Marx Archives.

17. See article "Sulzberger," *United Synagogue Recorder* 3, no. 3 (July 1923): 6 f.

18. Letter, JTS Marx Archives, May 4, 1916.

19. Letter, ibid., June 5, 1924.

20. *JTS Register*, 1924, pp. 122 f.

21. "Professor Alexander Marx," *United Synagogue Recorder*, 8, no. 1 (February 1928): 2 f.

22. Letter, JTS Marx Archives, March 11, 1930.

23. Adler, *Selected letters*, II:73 f.

24. Cyrus Adler, *Louis Marshall: A Biographical Sketch* (New York, 1931), p. 4.

25. For more information, see Charles Reznikoff, ed., *Louis Marshall: Champion of Liberty; Selected Papers and Addresses*, 2 vols. (Philadelphia, 1937).

26. Ibid., II: 884

27. Ibid., p. 867.

28. Ibid., I:xxii.

29. Ginzberg letters, January 5 and 14, 1927, JTS Archives. On the role of Marshall within Temple Emanu-El, see Ronald B. Sobel, "A History of New York's Temple Emanu-El: The Second Half Century" (Ph.D. diss., New York University, 1980), pp. 180 f. and 222 f.

30. Reznikoff, *Champion of Liberty*, II: 886 f.

31. Ibid., pp. 881 f.

32. On the history of Yeshiva, see Gilbert Klaperman, *The Story of Yeshiva University, the First Jewish University in America* (New York, 1969).

33. Reznikoff, *Champion of Liberty*, II: 891 f.

34. Ibid., p. 894 n.

35. Marx, "The Library," p. 119.

36. For a biographical sketch, see David Philipson, "Hyman Gerson Enelow," *American Jewish Yearbook*, vol. 36 (1934), pp. 25 f.

37. *Menorat Ha-Maor by Rabbi Israel Ibn Al Nakawa*, 4 vols. (New York, 1929–32); *Mishnah of Rabbi Eliezer; or, The Midrash of Thirty-Two Hermeneutic Rules* (New York, 1933).

38. Israel Davidson, ed., *Essays and Studies in Memory of Linda R. Miller* (New York, 1938).

39. Letter, JTS Lieberman Archives, February 12, 1934.

40. Marx, "The Library," pp. 99 f.

41. For an overview, see Michael A. Meyer, "The Refugee Scholars Project of the Hebrew Union College," in *Bicentennial Festschrift for Jacob Rader Marcus*, ed. Bertram Wallace Korn (Waltham and New York, 1976) pp. 359 f.

42. From a letter to the writer, dated December 12, 1985. In the United States, Gruenewald also served as president of the Leo Baeck Institute, New York, from 1955 to 1985.

CHAPTER FOUR

1. News release, JTS, May 2, 1940.

2. Cyrus Adler, *Selected Letters*, ed. Ira Robinson, 2 vols. (Philadelphia and New York, 1985), II:72.

3. For a bibliography, see *A Bibliography of the Writings of Louis Finkelstein* (New York, 1977), and Jacob Kabakoff, *Hadoar*, June 28, 1985, pp. 488 f.

4. Letter, JTS Marx Archives.

5. Interview with the author, September 3, 1985.

6. Letter, JTS Marx Archives.

7. Ibid., July 21, 1942.

8. *Hadoar*, October 5, 1945, pp. 904 f.; Eli Ginzberg, *Keeper of the Law: Louis Ginzberg* (Philadelphia, 1966), p. 144; and Herbert Parzen, *Architects of Conservative Judaism* (New York, 1964), p. 200.

9. *Proceedings of the Rabbinical Assembly of America*, vol. 9, pp. 193 f.

10. Ibid., p. 218.

11. For a brief history, see A. S. W. Rosenbach, "The Seminary Museum," in *The Jewish Theological Seminary of America: Semicentennial Volume* (New York, 1939), pp. 144 f.

12. Letter, JTS Marx Archives.

13. For further details, see Herman Dicker, *Piety and Perseverance: Jews from the Carpathian Mountains* (New York, 1981), pp. 96 f.

14. See Baron's introductions to (a) "Tentative List of Jewish Cultural Treasures in Axis-occupied Countries," *Supplement to Jewish Social Studies* 8, no. 1 (New York, 1946); (b) "Tentative List of Jewish Educational Institutions in Axis-occupied Countries," ibid., no. 3; (c) "Tentative List of Jewish Periodicals in Axis-occupied Countries," ibid., vol. 9, no. 3. Additional information from interview of Salo Baron by the author, February 12, 1986.

15. Leslie I. Poste, *The Development of U.S. Protection of Libraries and Archives in Europe during World War II* (Fort Gordon, Ga., 1958), pp. 298 f.

16. See Appendix B, "Distribution of Heirless Cultural Property: Offenbach Archival Depot, Jewish Cultural Reconstruction Foundation."

17. Shlomo Shunami, *About Libraries and Librarianship* (Hebrew) (Jerusalem, 1969), pp. 53 f.

18. See Herman Dicker, *Creativity, Holocaust, Reconstruction: Jewish Life in Wuerttemberg, Past and Present* (New York, 1984), p. 131.

19. *Talmud* (Munich and Heidelberg, 1948). Rabbi Snieg's dedication also includes thanks to Rabbi Philip S. Bernstein, advisor on Jewish affairs at U.S. Army Headquarters, Professor Samuel Sar of the Central Orthodox Committee, and Rabbi Solomon Shapiro of the American Joint Distribution Committee.

20. Rabbi Gruenewald was associated with the Seminary as a refugee scholar, as described in chapter 3. The president of the Leo Baeck Institute, New York, from 1955 to 1985, he was interviewed by the author on January 21, 1986. The word *Klaus* (German *Klause*) is derived from the medieval Latin *clusa* ("cloister"), and in Jewish history came to mean a House of Study.

21. Gerson D. Cohen, Foreword to *The Rothschild Mahzor, 1492* (New York, 1983), pp. 7 f.

22. Library report, May 6, 1947, JTS Marx Archives.

23. Letter, ibid.

24. Ibid.

CHAPTER FIVE

1. Report to overseers meeting, January 21, 1951, p. 8 (JTS Archives, Administrative file).

2. They were so named because a bibliographical insert was typed on the reverse side of the notorious newspaper *Stuermer* ("Stormer").

3. Memorandum, January 5, 1951 (JTS Archives, Administrative file).

4. Library report, January 29, 1954, to March 31, 1954 (JTS Archives, loc. cit.).

5. Memorandum, March 1955 (JTS Archives, loc. cit.).

6. From interview of Gerson D. Cohen by Herman Dicker, November 7, 1985.

7. Nahum M. Sarna to Herman Dicker, February 3, 1986.

8. Ibid.

9. Library report, May 15, 1959, to September 30, 1959, p. 1 (JTS Archives, Administrative file).

10. The Tauber report appeared in a mimeographed edition entitled: Maurice F. Tauber, "A Report of the Library of the Jewish Theological Seminary" (prepared at the request of the Administration of the Jewish Theological Seminary, New York, 1959).

11. The English title of Dr. Schmelzer's Hebrew dissertation is "The Poetical Works of Isaac Ibn Ghayyat."

CHAPTER SEVEN

1. *Jewish Book Annual* 21 (1963–64): 53–59.

Bibliography

Adler, Cyrus. *Jacob Schiff, His Life and Letters*, 2 vols. New York, 1928.
——. *Louis Marshall: A Biographical Sketch*. New York, 1931.
——. *I Have Considered the Days*. Philadelphia, 1945.
——. *Selected Letters*. Edited by Ira Robinson. 2 vols. Philadelphia and New York, 1985.
Ben-Horin, Meir. "Solomon Schechter to Judge Mayer Sulzberger." Part I: "Letters from the Pre-Seminary Period (1895–1901)." *Jewish Social Studies*, 25, no. 4 (October 1963): 249 f. Part II: "Letters from the Seminary Period (1902–1915)." *ibid.*, 27, no. 2 (April 1965): 75 f. Supplements to Parts I and II: *ibid.* 30, no. 4 (October 1968): 262 f.
Bentwich, Norman. *Solomon Schechter: A Biography*. New York, 1938.
Cohen, Naomi. *Encounter with Emancipation*. Philadelphia, 1984.
Commission on European Jewish Cultural Reconstruction. "Tentative List of Jewish Cultural Treasures in Axis-Occupied Countries." Supplement to *Jewish Social Studies* 8, nos. 1 and 3 (1946); 9, no. 3 (1947).
Davis, Moshe. *The Emergence of Conservative Judaism*. New York, 1963.
Ginzberg, Eli. *Keeper of the Law: Louis Ginzberg*. Philadelphia, 1966.
Gordis, Robert. *Understanding Conservative Judaism*. New York, 1978.
Greenberg, Simon. *Foundations of a Faith*. New York, 1967.
Jewish Theological Seminary Association. *Proceedings of Biennial Conventions I–VIII*. New York, 1888–1902.
Jewish Theological Seminary of America. *Biennial Report 1902–1904*. New York, 1906.
——. *Semicentennial Volume*. New York, 1939.
——. *Register*. New York, 1904–82.
——. *Academic Bulletin*. New York, 1976–86.
——. *Reports for Overseers*. New York, 1962–75.
——. *Reports from Chancellor Gerson D. Cohen*. New York, 1976–84.

Marx, Alexander. *Studies in Jewish History and Booklore*. New York, 1944.

———. *Essays in Jewish Biography*. Philadelphia, 1947.

Parzen, Herbert. *Architects of Conservative Judaism*. New York, 1964.

Poste, Leslie I. *The Development of U.S. Protection of Libraries and Archives in Europe during World War II*. Fort Gordon, Ga., 1958.

Reznikoff, Charles, ed. *Louis Marshall: Champion of Liberty, Selected Papers and Addresses*. 2 vols. Philadelphia, 1937.

Rosenblum, Herbert. *Conservative Judaism*. New York, 1983.

Schechter, Solomon: *Seminary Addresses and Other Papers*. New York, 1959.

———. *Studies in Judaism*, second series. Philadelphia, 1908.

Shargel, Baila R. *Practical Dreamer: Israel Friedlaender and the Shaping of American Judaism*. New York, 1986.

Tauber, Maurice F. "A Report of the Library of the Jewish Theological Seminary." Mimeographed. New York, 1959.

Index